# FACING REALITY

# Facing Reality

## TWO TRUTHS
## ABOUT RACE IN AMERICA

*Charles Murray*

NEW YORK · LONDON

First American edition published in 2021 by Encounter Books,
an activity of Encounter for Culture and Education, Inc.,
a nonprofit, tax-exempt corporation.
Encounter Books website address: www.encounterbooks.com

Manufactured in the United States and printed on
acid-free paper. The paper used in this publication meets
the minimum requirements of ANSI/NISO Z39.48–1992
(R 1997) (*Permanence of Paper*).

FIRST AMERICAN EDITION

LIBRARY OF CONGRESS CATALOGING-IN-PUBLICATION DATA

Names: Murray, Charles A., author.
Title: Facing Reality: Two Truths about Race in America /
Charles Murray.
Description: First American edition. | New York, New York:
Encounter Books, 2021. | Includes bibliographical references
and index. |
Identifiers: LCCN 2021000549 (print) | LCCN 2021000550 (ebook) |
ISBN 9781641771979 (hardcover) | ISBN 9781641771986 (ebook)
Subjects: LCSH: Racism—United States. | Race. | Intelligence levels—
United States. | Crime and race—United States. | Discrimination in
law enforcement—United States. | United States—Race relations. |
United States—Social policy.
Classification: LCC E184.A1 M8955 2021 (print) |
LCC E184.A1 (ebook) |
DDC 305.800973—dc23
LC record available at https://lccn.loc.gov/2021000549
LC ebook record available at https://lccn.loc.gov/2021000550

# CONTENTS

# Note to the Reader

THE EMPIRICAL ASSERTIONS in *Facing Reality* are not complicated in themselves, and in a reasonable world they would not be controversial. They are facts that we must face. It shouldn't take long to read them, and it won't. You can read the main text of *Facing Reality* over the course of an evening. Maybe two.

The story behind the facts is occasionally complicated, however, and aspects of the facts are controversial for understandable reasons, but different readers will have different reservations. Some of you will be comfortable accepting arrest data as quantitative evidence of criminal behavior but doubt that IQ tests tell us anything worth knowing. Others will be familiar with the basics of IQ but suspicious of anything the police tell us. The endnotes present additional evidence or further explanation of technical issues. Standard documentation of sources, still more elaboration of technical issues, and downloadable databases have been posted online at encounterbooks.com/books/facing-reality.

# Introduction

I DECIDED TO WRITE this book in the summer of 2020 because of my dismay at the disconnect between the rhetoric about "systemic racism" and the facts. The uncritical acceptance of that narrative by the nation's elite news media amounted to an unwillingness to face reality.

By *facts*, I mean what Senator Daniel Patrick Moynihan meant: "Everyone is entitled to his own opinion but not to his own facts." By *reality*, I mean what the science fiction novelist Philip Dick meant: "Reality is that which, when you stop believing in it, doesn't go away."

I do not dispute evidence of the racism that persists in American life. Rather, I reject the portrayal of American society and institutions as systemically racist and saturated in White privilege. What follows is a data-driven discussion of realities that make America a more complicated and much less racist nation than its radical critics describe.

Of the many facts about race that are ignored, two above all, long since documented beyond reasonable doubt, must be brought into the open and incorporated into the way we think about why American society is the way it is and what can be done through public policy to improve it.

The first is that American Whites, Blacks, Latinos, and Asians, *as groups*, have different means and distributions of cognitive ability. The second is that American Whites, Blacks, Latinos, and Asians, *as groups*, have different rates of violent crime. Allegations of systemic racism in policing, education, and the workplace cannot be assessed without dealing with the reality of group differences.

There is a reason that reality is ignored. The two facts make people excruciatingly uncomfortable. To raise them is to be considered a racist and hateful person. What's more, these facts have been distorted and exploited for malign purposes by racist and hateful people.

What then is the point of writing about them? Aren't some realities better ignored? The answer goes to a much deeper problem than false accusations of systemic racism. We are engaged in a struggle for America's soul. Facing reality is essential if that struggle is to be won.

# The American Creed Imperiled

*It has been our fate as a nation
not to have ideologies, but to be one.*
RICHARD HOFSTADTER

AMERICA'S FOUNDING IDEALS – America's soul – used to be called the American creed. The creed's origin is the first sentence of the second paragraph of the Declaration of Independence: "We hold these truths to be self-evident, that all men are created equal, that they are endowed by their Creator with certain unalienable Rights...." In Samuel Huntington's words, the creed embodies "the political principles of liberty, equality, democracy, individualism, human rights, the rule of law, and private property."[1]

Europeans who looked with hope to America in the nineteenth century grasped a simpler meaning: In America, they would be the equals of anyone else – equal before the law and possessing the same inherent human dignity as anyone else. In America, they would be judged on who they were as individuals, not by what social class they came from or how they worshipped God. That promise drew immigrants by the millions who believed that in America you could go as far as your own hard work and talent would take you.

Our history is riddled with failures to achieve our ideal,

1

starting with the Declaration's failure to condemn slavery, but the American creed itself has always been powerful. Over the course of the nineteenth century, both the abolitionist and the feminist movements drew their moral authority and their ultimate successes from appeals to live up to the American creed. In the early 1940s, writing in his landmark book, *An American Dilemma*, the Swedish economist Gunnar Myrdal capitalized the term and marveled at the creed's continuing universality. "Even a poor and uneducated white person in some isolated and backward rural region in the Deep South who is violently prejudiced against the Negro and intent upon depriving him of civic rights and human independence, has also a whole compartment in his valuation sphere housing the entire American Creed of liberty, equality, justice, and fair opportunity for everybody," he wrote. The creed was what made America *America*.

Myrdal was writing a decade before the civil rights movement gained momentum in the mid-1950s. The most dramatic single moment of that crusade, Martin Luther King's "I have a dream" speech on the Washington Mall on August 28, 1963, evoked the American creed from start to finish.

"In a sense we've come to our nation's capital to cash a check," King said near the opening. "When the architects of our republic wrote the magnificent words of the Constitution and the Declaration of Independence, they were signing a promissory note to which every American was to fall heir."

Reaching the peroration, he proclaimed his first dream, that "the nation will rise up and live out the true meaning of its creed: 'We hold these truths to be self-evident, that all men are created equal.'"

The iconic line from the speech, King's dream that his four children would one day "not be judged by the color of their skin but by the content of their character," was a reification of the creed.

That speech was the capstone to a compelling appeal that had raised the consciousness – the phrase is appropriate, for once – of White America over the course of the preceding decade.

You have to be quite old to remember how uncomplicated it seemed to many of us, White and Black alike, in 1963. African Americans had been wronged for centuries, during slavery and after. It was time to set things right. Ten months later, the Civil Rights Act of 1964 was signed by Lyndon Johnson. It had passed by overwhelming margins in both houses of Congress, with almost all of the opposition coming from Southern members.

There. We had done it. We had set things right.

Some who voted for the bill had misgivings about a few provisions. Titles II and III, banning race discrimination in public accommodations and public facilities, entailed obvious restrictions on freedom of association. Title VII, on equal employment opportunity, made employers vulnerable to legal scrutiny if they didn't think in terms of groups. But in the floor debates and in the press, these provisions were described as one-time exceptions justified by the unique injustice done to African Americans. It's not as if the act would seriously infringe on traditional American freedoms. As Hubert Humphrey, the Senate's leading liberal, put it when discussing the section on employment discrimination, the wording of the bill "does not limit the employer's freedom to hire, fire, promote, or demote for any reason – or no reason – as long as his action is not based on race, color, religion, national origin, or sex." The act had to be a good and necessary thing. As a college junior at the time, I certainly thought so.

Nonetheless, a philosophical wedge had been driven between those who wanted strict adherence to the ideal of treating people as individuals, equal before the law, and those who advocated group-based policies as a way to achieve social justice. The Civil Rights Act of 1964 had added a caveat to the creed.

Less than a year later, President Lyndon Johnson announced "the next and profound stage of the battle for civil rights" – namely, "not just equality as a right and a theory but equality as a fact and equality as a result." It marked the beginning of a process whereby the founding ideals of the American creed were recast as the struggle for social justice. Title VII of the law was interpreted as permitting preferential consideration for African Americans in admissions to colleges and in employment. And it turned out to be not merely a one-time exception to remedy a unique injustice. Group-based exceptions for special treatment were widened to include not only women but also the physically disabled, the mentally disabled, the elderly, and eventually homosexuals. The gap between liberal and conservative interpretations of the creed widened as well. The term itself fell out of use.

The twenty-first century saw the growth of a new ideology that repudiated the American creed altogether. It began in academia as intersectionality and critical race theory conjoined with a bastardized vision of socialism. By 2016, it exerted significant influence within the left wing of the Democratic Party. As I write, the new ideology still goes by several names. "Woke" originated within the African American community. "Critical race theory" and "anti-racism" are the most widely used terms. But there's one label that covers it all: identity politics.

At the heart of identity politics is the truth that "who we are" as individuals is importantly shaped by our race and sex. I've been aware of that truth as I wrote this book – my perspective as a straight White male has affected the text, sometimes consciously and sometimes inadvertently. But identity politics does not limit itself to acknowledging the importance of race and sex to our personae. The core premise of identity politics is that individuals are *inescapably defined* by the groups into which they were born – principally (but not exclusively) by race and sex – and that this understanding must shape our politics. Identity politics turns the American creed on its head. Treating people as individuals is considered immoral because it ignores our history of racism and sexism. Remedying America's systemic racism and omnipresent White privilege requires that people of color be treated preferentially. The power of the state not only may legitimately be used to this end, it must be so used, and sweepingly.

I didn't take identity politics seriously for a long time. I thought that the academy was once again indulging its fondness for recreational radicalism. Surely no one outside academia except the extreme left would pay much attention. I was wrong. I had underestimated the extent to which today's academia and today's elite media share the same worldview. I had underestimated the intolerance of dissent that went with the movement, and how effectively that intolerance could stifle opposition from moderate liberals.

In 2019, the campaign season for the Democratic presidential nomination began. By the end of the year it was clear that identity politics had become the consensus ideology of the left wing of the Democratic Party, not just the most extreme elements. Some of the Democratic candidates openly embraced identity politics. Others were more moderate and probably harbored reservations, but no major candidate for the nomination challenged identity politics aggressively.

When the protests and riots over the death of George Floyd erupted in the summer of 2020, identity politics demonstrated how far it had spread and how much influence it wielded not only over the Democratic Party and academia, but over corporate America too, as famous companies scrambled to condemn their own White privilege and promised to make amends. The new administration came to office in January 2021 with the support of American elites who had largely accepted that the ideals of colorblindness and America as a melting pot were not just outdated, they were evidence of the racism still embedded in the White consciousness. Within a week of his inauguration, President Biden signed four executive orders intended to promote "racial equity," promising that "we're going to make strides to end systemic racism, and every branch of the White House and the federal government will be part of that." His appointments to subcabinet posts and regulatory agencies are consistent with that rhetoric.

In some ways, there's nothing new here. The Biden administration is acting on an assumption that has been incorporated into law for more than fifty years: It is appropriate for the government to play racial favorites, to dispense favors and penalties according to the group to which individuals belong. My view is that this position has proved to be toxic. It is based on the premise that all groups are equal in the ways that shape economic, social, and political outcomes for groups and that therefore all differences in group outcomes are artificial and indefensible. That premise is factually wrong. Hence this book about race differences in cognitive ability and criminal behavior.

I am aware of the dangers of being misread. I am not talking about racial superiority or inferiority, but about differences in group averages and overlapping distributions. Differences in averages do not affect the abilities of any individual. They should not affect our approach, positively or negatively, to any person we meet. But experience has taught me how hard it is for people to accept those assurances.

I am also aware of a paradox: I want America to return to the ideal of treating people as individuals, so I have to

6

write a book that treats Americans as groups. But there's no way around it. Those of us who want to defend the American creed have been unwilling to say openly that races have significant group differences. Since we have been unwilling to say that, we have been defenseless against claims that racism is to blame for unequal outcomes. What else could it be? We have been afraid to answer candidly.

Because we have not talked openly about group differences, we have kidded ourselves that the differences are temporary and can be made to go away. The next big push, whether it takes the form of No Child Left Behind in 2001 or a campaign to root out systemic racism in 2021, will change things. We've been saying that since the War on Poverty in 1965. It has allowed us to evade our moral obligation to treat others as individuals even though mean differences between groups are a reality and will be with us indefinitely.

I've been having conversations about that moral obligation for decades. It has been disquieting to see how few people can make themselves confront it. "The differences *must* be temporary. If they aren't ... but they *must* be." Discarding that crutch is essential. *The more intractable the group differences, the more imperative the moral obligation.*

This book is written for all the people with whom I've had those disquieting conversations and the millions of others who think that group differences *must* be temporary. I've been unable to discern an ideological tilt. Well-meaning people on the right are as uncomfortable confronting the reality of group differences as well-meaning people on the left. But one audience is a special priority for me: people on the center-left who are liberals in the tradition that extended from FDR through Bill Clinton and included Senator Joe Biden. I suspect that any liberals who have gotten this far are wondering if I can possibly be serious: Can't Murray see that America's problems are coming from the radical right, the people who stormed the Capitol two weeks before Biden's inauguration?

That is partly true. What's happening on the right is half of the national crisis that threatens America's soul. But the other half is what's happening with identity politics on the left. If you are on the center left, the material in this book is unlikely to be treated accurately in the newspapers you read, the blogs you follow, your social media feeds, or the news that you watch or listen to.

Be assured that nothing in this book will challenge your political principles with which I disagree – there's nothing here promoting my libertarian views on freedom or small government. I continue to hold those views, but in this book I argue from a center-right position, aiming to make common cause with people of other political persuasions in restoring an element of the American creed on which we agree. For whatever has happened with the progressive left, the importance of equality before the law and of treating people as individuals has historically been at the core of American liberal principles – just as it has been at the core of American conservative principles, no matter what has happened with the Trumpian right.

As for the realities I describe, there's no way to sugarcoat them, and I decided not to try. But having described the realities we must face, I can try to convey the peril we are in if we ignore them. That is the subject of the concluding chapter.

CHAPTER TWO

# Multiracial America

I NEED TO BEGIN with some facts about America's racial
and ethnic make-up. Most of us are wrong. For example,
most Americans estimate that Blacks and Latinos are each
around 30 percent of the population.[1] Not even close. The
Census Bureau's figures as of 2019 were 12.8 percent for
Blacks and 18.4 percent for Latinos.

Table 1 below shows the racial and ethnic breakdown of
the American population as reported in the American
Community Survey (ACS) for 2019.

Whether this profile bears any resemblance to your
daily experience of America depends on where you live. If
you live in a city of half a million people or more, it probably does. Otherwise, probably not. If you live in Corpus
Christi, the percentage of Latinos in the table is far too low.
If you live in Savannah, the percentage of Blacks is far too
low. If you live in Fargo, the percentage of Whites is far too
low. If you live in Silicon Valley, the percentage of East
Asians is far too low.

Table 1
America's Detailed Racial and Ethnic Profile as of 2019

|  | Non-Latino | Latino |
|---|---|---|
| White | 60.0% | 12.1% |
| Black | 12.4% | 0.4% |
| East Asian | 2.4% | 0.0% |
| South Asian | 1.5% | 0.0% |
| Filipino/Pacific Islander | 1.1% | 0.0% |
| Native American | 0.7% | 0.2% |
| Southeast Asian | 0.6% | 0.0% |
| Other Asian | 0.1% | 0.1% |
| Other Single Race | 0.3% | 4.7% |
| White & Black | 0.7% | 0.1% |
| White & Native American | 0.5% | 0.1% |
| White & Asian | 0.5% | 0.1% |
| Other Combination | 0.8% | 0.6% |
| TOTAL | 81.6% | 18.4% |

## NOMENCLATURE

Should I refer to the groups in Table 1 as races? As ethnicities? Both? The question is particularly loaded in an age when race is widely argued to be a social construct – an artificial classification that marginalizes minorities but lacks a meaningful genetic foundation. Geneticists have dealt with this problem by dispensing with both *race* and *ethnicity*, and instead using the word *population*. They have found that they can accurately calibrate people's mix of ancestral heritages, whether they are popularly understood as races or ethnicities, by examining patterns of genetic variants. That's why commercial genetic testing companies such as 23andMe and AncestryDNA can, in return for a fee, tell you the breakdown of your own racial heritage. The level of detail that geneticists can achieve depends on the number of genetic variants they include in the analysis.

"Who are you?" racially and ethnically has different answers at different levels of specificity, and this is an excellent reason not to think in terms of races. Yet the census data tell us that 96.6 percent of us self-identify with a single race. This unrealistically high percentage can be seen as a common-sense compromise between genetic precision and cultural reality.

Taken as a group, self-identified Whites have complicated mixes of European ethnicities, but little racial ambiguity. In a large study based on 23andMe data, they had a mean of 98.6 percent European ancestry, 0.2 percent Native American ancestry, and 0.2 percent African ancestry, with the rest being "Other."

Self-identified Blacks in America have a significant White admixture – something that has roots in slavery and has been known anecdotally throughout American history. Starting in the 1950s, studies have attempted to measure that admixture, with estimates of mean European ancestry for Blacks ranging from 7 percent to 23 percent. The best estimate of the current ethnic mix, produced by the Health and Retirement Study, which used a nationally representative sample of Black Americans, is 82.1 percent Black, 16.7 percent White, and 1.2 percent Native American.

Neither of the previous studies included Asians. Since a high proportion of today's American Asians are recent immigrants who arrived directly from their ancestral countries, it is likely that Asian ancestry among self-identified Asians is extremely high.

Self-identified Latinos can be of any race if their families came to the United States from Latin America. That's why the Census Bureau asks two separate questions in its annual American Community Survey: Whether the respondent is ethnically Latino or Hispanic and what race the respondent identifies with. Note that the Census Bureau now gives equal billing to both labels. I choose Latino.

In the 2019 ACS, 66 percent of all people who self-identified as Latino also self-identified as White, while 29 percent self-identified either as "Other Single Race" or as a combination of two or more races *not* including White, Black, Asian, Filipino, or Polynesian.

A fine-grained breakout of the ACS data on ethnic heritage gives clues about what "other" race that 29 percent of Latinos have in mind. Many Latinos who say they are of another single race or a combination of unnamed races are thinking of a specific people indigenous to Latin America – Mayan, for example – or are treating Mestizo as a race. *Mestizo* is defined as the descendent of a mating of a European and a person indigenous to Latin America. But that mating may have occurred at any time since 1492. People with varying amounts of Spanish and indigenous ancestry have been intermarrying for so long that it is reasonable for them to believe that their racial composition now amounts to a distinct category.

The answers to the Census Bureau's questions are consistent with the 23andMe genetic findings about Latinos. In that sample, the self-identified Latinos showed 65.1 percent European ancestry, 6.2 percent African ancestry, and 18.0 percent Native American ancestry, leaving 10.7 percent for the rest. But these numbers are far from evenly distributed across the self-identified Latinos. Approximately 60 percent of them had no African or Native American ancestry, meaning that most of those 60 percent had to have very high proportions of European ancestry (the published data don't permit me to be more precise than that). Meanwhile, Native American ancestry is by definition pre-Columbian indigenous ancestry. Combine the 18.0 percent average Native American ancestry with a substantial portion of the 10.7 percent unidentified ancestry, and the implication (consistent with the self-reports) is that a large proportion of Latinos have a substantial share of indigenous ancestry – they are Mestizos.

All this means that it is problematic to lump Latinos into a single group when analyzing either cognitive ability or crime. People who self-identify as Latino span the range from those who have been living in what is now the United States for centuries to first-generation immigrants; from Latinos who are genetically 100 percent European to Latinos who are 100 percent descendants of a specific indigenous pre-Columbian population.

This brings me to my decisions about nomenclature. Almost all of us have some mixture of ethnic heritages, but more than 97 percent of us nonetheless identify with a single race that has a geographic origin. Furthermore, while it is appropriate for geneticists to discard the word *race* because of its semantic baggage, that same semantic baggage is an important aspect of American life.

If I don't use the geneticists' solution, speaking of various *populations* in America, should I refer instead to races or ethnicities? *Race* works reasonably well for Whites, Blacks, and Asians. It doesn't accurately characterize Latinos. Rather than repeat "race or ethnicity" a few hundred times in the rest of the book, I decided to use *race* for Latinos as well, with the understanding that for them it is inadequate.

What about the labels for the four populations that will be at the center of attention: White, Black, Latino, and Asian? When I'm discussing race in its political and cultural context, those labels are appropriate, and I will return to them in the concluding chapter with its intensely political and cultural analysis.

I'm unhappy with the labels *White* and *Black* for the four intervening chapters that discuss race differences in cognitive ability and crime. One of my goals is to demonstrate that it is possible to discuss these topics dispassionately, which among other things means stripping them of as many political and cultural distractions as possible. My message in those four chapters is that the *existence* of differences in test scores and the *existence* of differences in crime rates are facts that we do not have the option of denying. The existence of these differences has certain built-in effects on socioeconomic reality that we do not have the option of denying. The facts and the reality remain true no matter what the causes of the differences might be or one's policy preferences for dealing with them. I hope you will come to agree that focusing on what *is* is clarifying.

*White* and *Black* get in the way of that dispassion. The label *White* evokes one set of ancillary meanings for the "woke" and another for White nationalists. Capitalized *Black* is the latest in a series of labels that have been considered respectful and correct at one time or another – colored, Negro, Afro-American, black, African American – each of which evokes its own historical era. Whites pushed for the label *Native American*, but most of the people it was intended to please still call themselves Indians. I would like to jar us loose from the connotations that are associated with those labels to make it easier to look at some inflammatory issues with at least a little more detachment.

Referring to populations A, B, C, and D would make the discussion too hard to follow. Instead, I substitute *European* for *White*, *African* for *Black*, *Latin* for *Latino*, and *Amerindian* for *Native American*. *Asian* remains *Asian*.

While writing those four chapters, I was often tempted to revert to the usual labels entirely. I suspect that many of you will often (or always) wish I had done so. There is something intuitively wrong about calling American Whites *Europeans* when American Whites are so clearly not like Europeans in Europe.[2] The same is true of American Blacks compared to Africans living in Africa, American

Latins living in the United States compared to Latins living in Latin America, and, for that matter, American Asians compared to Asians living in Asia. But every time I wished I could write simply *Whites* or *Blacks*, and then asked myself what would happen if I did, the answer was that *Whites* or *Blacks* would let the semantic baggage associated with those labels affect the interpretation of the sentence. Better that you be jarred, I decided, if it might improve my chances that you understand the sentence as I intend it to be understood.

## AMERICA'S RACIAL PROFILE THEN AND NOW

America's racial history can be summarized in a few sentences. The United States saw sweeping ethnic changes in its population from the 1840s through World War I, as successive waves of Irish, German, Scandinavian, Italian, and Eastern European immigrants arrived. But, with the exception of comparatively small Chinese and Japanese immigrations to the West Coast, all of those new groups were European. Thus America experienced great ethnic roiling during the nineteenth century (hostility toward new European ethnicities was widespread and virulent) but only small changes in its racial profile until the late 1960s. From the first census in 1790 through the 1850 census, the population within America's settled regions was 82–84 percent European and the rest was African. Subsequent tides of immigration increased the proportion of Europeans. As of the 1960 census, America was about 87 percent European, 11 percent African, something more than 1 percent Latin, and something less than 1 percent Asian.[3] America was effectively a biracial country with one race overwhelmingly dominant in numbers as well as dominant politically, economically, and culturally.

Then, in 1965, Congress passed the Immigration and Nationality Act. America changed rapidly. Applying my nomenclature and rules for classifying Latins, the American population profile as of 2019 looked like this:

| | |
|---|---|
| European | 60.0% |
| Latin | 17.9% |
| African | 12.8% |
| Asian | 5.7% |
| Amerindian | 0.7% |
| Pacific Islander | 0.2% |
| Other | 2.8% |

Latins and Asians are now many multiples of their 1960 proportions. The Latin population is about 40 percent larger than the African population. The Asian population is approaching half the African population. Europeans are still a majority but not even close to their former dominance.

## The Geography of Multiracial America

Seen at the national level, the changes in America's racial profile after the passage of the 1965 immigration act were gigantic. When we look around the country, the changes have been gigantic in some places but minor in others. Big cities have been affected much more than the rest of the country.

### *Big-City America*

America's big cities have been transformed by immigration over the past several decades. In 1960, New York was the most cosmopolitan city in America but its population was still more than three-quarters European. New York City went from 77 percent European in 1960 to 32 percent in 2019. That's a transformation by any definition.

Other major cities changed even more than New York did. From 1960 to 2019, Los Angeles went from 85 percent European to 29 percent; Chicago went from 82 to 34 percent; Houston went from 77 to 23 percent. All the rhetoric about the racial diversity of America is true – for big cities.

I am defining *big-city America* as urban areas with populations of 500,000 or more in a contiguous urban environment (which often does not correspond to the legal boundaries of the city). There are fifty-two of them, all located in the Lower Forty-Eight. The fifty-two urban areas take up only 1 percent of the Lower Forty-Eight's land mass, but they contain 70 percent of its Asians, 54 percent of its Latins, and 52 percent of its Africans. No race has a majority of big-city America's population. Europeans amount to 45 percent, followed by Latins at 25 percent, Africans at 17 percent, and Asians of all varieties at 9 percent.

The total population of big-city America is 127 million, representing 39 percent of the total population of the Lower Forty-Eight. That's a lot, but it also means that a majority of Americans live in rural areas, towns, or cities with urban populations of fewer than 500,000. They live in the other 99 percent of the Lower Forty-Eight's land area.

### America Outside the Big Cities

Since big-city America contains so many of our Africans, Latins, and Asians, the percentages for America outside the big cities are much different. The European percentage rises from 45 to 71 percent, while the Latin and African percentages fall to 14 percent and 10 percent respectively. Asians are rare outside urban America – just 3 percent of the population. Figure 1 in the color insert is a map of the Lower Forty-Eight color-coded as follows:

Blue represents zip codes in which Europeans are at least 50 percent of the population and no single minority is 25 percent. The darker the blue, the higher the European percentage.

Red represents zip codes in which Africans are at least 25 percent of the population and the largest minority. The darker the red, the higher the African percentage.

Orange represents zip codes in which Latins are at least 25 percent of the population and the largest minority. The darker the orange, the higher the Latin percentage.

Green represents zip codes in which Amerindians are at least 25 percent of the population and the largest minority. The darker the green, the higher the Amerindian percentage.

Gray represents zip codes in which Asians are at least 25 percent of the population and the largest minority. The darker the gray, the higher the Asian percentage.

Purple represents zip codes in big-city America.

The map shows three obvious geographic groupings of American zip codes: Africans in the states that once formed the Confederacy; Latins in the southern half of Florida, the Southwest, much of California, and a few other western concentrations; and Europeans everywhere else.

A less obvious grouping is the archipelago of zip codes with at least 25 percent Amerindians located on or near Amerindian reservations in the Southwest and Mountain West. A handful of gray zip codes that are at least 25 percent Asian, mostly in Silicon Valley and east of San Francisco, are invisible at the scale of this map. The zip codes associated with Amerindian reservations are geographically large but sparsely populated, containing just 530,046 self-identified Amerindians. The gray zip codes that you cannot see contain 390,843 Asians.

The map drives home how radically differently Americans in various parts of the country have experienced the transformation in the national racial profile. Big-city America is authentically multiracial, far more so than the major cities of Europe or Asia. The Deep South is biracial, with a European majority and a large African minority, but hardly any Asians and relatively few Latins outside the big cities. The Southwest and California up through the Central Valley are also biracial, but with a different pair of races and an even larger minority, Latins being more than a third of the total population. In this part of America, outside the big cities and Silicon Valley, Asians and Africans are a few percent of the population. The geographically vast area where Europeans are still dominant is monoracial in a surprising number of towns and small cities, and elsewhere is no more multiracial than America as a whole was in 1960.

These are the bare bones of America's racial structure. I hope it is clear how poorly that structure fits the popular narrative. Put roughly, the narrative tells us that America is moving toward a multiracial society in which Europeans will soon be a minority and we all need to adjust in similar ways. The reality is that different parts of America have had widely varying experiences with a multiracial society and are moving toward even more different futures.

## CHAPTER THREE

# Race Differences in Cognitive Ability

MOST PEOPLE WHO call someone "smart" or "bright" or "intelligent" are talking about the quality that IQ tests measure. That quality is not virtue, merit, character, wisdom, or common sense. It is irrelevant to human worth. IQ denotes the mental agility that lets some people collate disparate bits of information and then infer and deduce from that information better than other people, whether the task is to decipher a corporate balance sheet, analyze *Middlemarch*, or determine why the car won't start. The quality measured by IQ tests assists people in figuring things out, both in their professions and in everyday life.

More technically, IQ tests are the best measure of the general mental factor known as $g$, which in turn is the most rigorously investigated construct in psychology.[1] In a field riddled with fads that are enthusiastically accepted initially but fail to pan out (recall the claims once made for the importance of self-esteem and stereotype threat),[2] the major findings produced by IQ tests have been replicated time and again over decades, with different instruments, for all kinds of populations tested in all kinds of conditions. The quantitative understanding of cognitive ability has the distinction of being at once a crowning achievement of psychology and widely criticized as pseudoscience.

The charges of pseudoscience have many sources.[3]

Some of these challenges need to be taken seriously. Is cognitive ability too complex to be represented by a single number? For some purposes, yes; for others, no. Are there multiple intelligences? There are certainly multiple talents, but it is possible to distinguish talents from cognitive ability both conceptually and statistically.[4] These and other questions are worth asking, and much has been learned from investigating them over the decades. But another source of resistance to accepting the validity of IQ tests is that the tests have persistently indicated different means and distributions of cognitive ability among races. Many people today consider this unacceptable – so unacceptable that it cannot possibly be true. And yet it is.

I have three contentions to defend:

> ➤ When Africans, Asians, Europeans, and Latins take tests that are related to cognitive ability, their group results have different means.

> ➤ Race differences between Africans and Europeans in cognitive test scores narrowed significantly during the 1970s and 1980s, but the narrowing stopped three decades ago.

> ➤ Scores on today's most widely used standardized tests, whether they are tests of cognitive ability or academic achievement, pass the central test of fairness: They do not underpredict the performance of lower-scoring groups in the classroom or on the job.

Each of these is a statement of fact. To understand the evidence for them and why that evidence has been so strenuously resisted for so long, some historical context may be useful – including ways in which my own work has intersected with that history.

## A Short History

Standardized tests with nationally representative samples didn't become part of the landscape until the second half of the twentieth century, and even then only slowly. As of the end of the 1950s, many school systems administered standardized achievement tests and many administered a written test of cognitive ability to eighth-graders as a resource for their high school guidance counselors. (Where I grew up, it wasn't called an IQ test and students never learned their scores.) The SAT was widely known, but only the small minority of high school seniors who wanted to go to a selective college needed to take it.

Race differences in cognitive ability – which in America then meant the difference between Europeans and Africans – were not a major issue. Teachers in integrated schools in the North knew that African students on average didn't perform as well as European students in the classroom, but the magnitude of the national difference was open to argument. All of the existing studies of African test scores had used small samples or large but unrepresentative samples.[5]

Differences in classroom performance didn't necessarily mean much anyway. The great majority of African students were in segregated schools in the South. The accounts of terrible school facilities and inadequate schooling for African children in the South were familiar to everyone. So were the problems that existed in de facto segregated urban schools in the North. It was assumed that better education for African children would shrink the performance gap to insignificance.

In 1960, the U.S. Office of Education sponsored a national survey known as Project Talent, intended to be the first scientifically planned national inventory of human talents, with a sample of 440,000 high school students. Assessing race differences had not been one of the goals of the project. It was then illegal to ask participants about their race, and the published results at the time did not mention any race differences. But information about race could be drawn from results in one-race schools (which were then common), and further information was obtained through follow-up surveys in later years. All this indicated a large racial difference. Exactly how large is uncertain, but it was around the equivalent of 19 to 23 IQ points.

Four years later, Section 402 of the Civil Rights Act of 1964 required the commissioner of the Office of Educa-tion to conduct a survey "concerning the lack of availabil-ity of equal educational opportunities for individuals by reason of race, color, religion, or national origin in public educational institutions." The sample was massive: 645,000 students in 4,000 schools. The report of the results, known as "the Coleman Report" after its principal investigator, the sociologist James S. Coleman, was submitted in July 1966. This was a pivotal event in social science, represent-ing the first important use of multivariate regression, a technique that has since become the workhorse of quanti-tative economic and sociological analysis.

The Coleman Report published the racial means on the study's cognitive test battery. Subsequent analyses refined the results, finding that the European–African difference was about 15 points for ninth-graders and 18 points for twelfth-graders, but the size of the difference in test scores was ignored in the midst of the consternation created by the Coleman Report's central conclusion that the quality of a school played almost no role in explaining the perfor-mance of African students. This was heresy – the point of the survey had been to prove that poor education was to blame for the problems of African students and better edu-cation would be the solution. But the Coleman Report found that the far more important factors were aspects of a student's family background.

The Coleman Report had no effect on policy – Congress had already passed the Elementary and Secondary Education Act in 1965, a year before the report was released – but among those who read and understood its analysis, the results were portentous. If you believed the Coleman analysis, you had reason to be skeptical that improvements in schooling would close the European–African gap in test scores.

For the rest of the 1960s and throughout the 1970s, race differences in cognitive ability were seldom part of the policy conversation. A notable exception was Arthur Jensen's 1969 article in the *Harvard Educational Review* arguing that educational programs were unlikely to close the gap because it was substantially genetic. But that was followed in 1972 by Christopher Jencks's *Inequality: A Reassessment of the Effect of Family and Schooling in America*, which made the case for environmental explanations of the gap. Policy analysts embraced Jencks's analysis and dismissed Jensen's. In any case, everyone knew that results of cognitive tests were irrelevant because the tests were so culturally biased against Africans.

As a policy analyst just beginning his career, I shared those positions. In 1977, for example, I was conducting an evaluation of a Chicago program to divert chronic male delinquents from reform schools. I spent a few weeks in the headquarters of the Juvenile Division of the Illinois Department of Corrections in St. Charles, Illinois, laboriously transferring information from each boy's record to my database. Each record included a score on the Stanford-Binet IQ test. Just two or three digits to write down. But almost all of the boys were African, so I didn't bother to do it – I knew those numbers were uninterpretable.

A few years later I read Arthur Jensen's *Bias in Mental*

*Testing*, documenting that the major tests were not biased against minorities. By the time I wrote *Losing Ground*, published in 1984, I no longer thought that African test scores were uninterpretable nor was I oblivious to the size of the differences in scores. Much of the chapter about education was devoted to discussing those differences. But I still thought that better education was the answer. Whereas I was pessimistic about the potential of federal social programs to do good in most arenas, I thought the one exception was school vouchers, especially for parents who were already actively engaged in overseeing their children's education. "I suggest that when we give such parents vouchers, we will observe substantial convergence of black and white test scores in a single generation," I wrote, confident that I was right.

During the 1980s, a number of new studies gave reason to think that things were getting better even without a school voucher program. When Richard Herrnstein and I were writing *The Bell Curve* in the early 1990s, we included encouraging signs that the European–African test-score difference was diminishing, though we were worried about signs that the narrowing had stalled.

By the time George W. Bush came to office in 2001, the stalling had continued for more than a decade. The new president, encouraged by his experience with educational reforms in Texas, got the support of Senator Ted Kennedy to pass the bipartisan No Child Left Behind bill, with its goal of bringing all – yes, *all* – children to proficiency in reading and math by 2014. Progress was to be measured by regular standardized tests, and schools that failed to make progress were subject to penalties.

The spotlight was now on K–12 test scores. The difficulties in raising test scores that had been worrying a comparatively few academics now became a topic in the media. In the first half of the 2000s, the public schools were convulsed with efforts to push borderline students over the threshold of proficiency. But the promised rise in African test scores failed to materialize. During the last half of the decade, most schools and the federal Department of Education alike tacitly admitted defeat.

The question of test-score differences had gotten more complicated during that decade. It was no longer a story of just African test scores, but Latin and Asian test scores as well. Latins also lagged behind Europeans, though by less than Africans did. But Asians did better than Europeans. A statement of the current race differences in cognitive ability is correspondingly more complicated.

## The Studies

Hundreds of studies have reported cognitive test scores for different races, but only a comparative handful are relevant to determining the best estimate of mean race differences in cognitive ability in the United States. To qualify for the inventory of studies I assembled, a study had to meet three criteria. First, it must have been designed to yield nationally representative results through its sample structure or through weights that could be attached to the participants' scores. Second, the study's cognitive tests must have included measures of both verbal and mathematical or visuospatial skills. Third, the persons in the sample in the study must have reached the onset of adolescence. Operationally, this worked out to samples in which the youngest member was at least twelve years old (with one exception for which a few members of the sample were only eleven). The reason for the age restriction is that my objective is to estimate mean race differences among adults. Race differences in cognitive ability increase significantly from infancy to childhood to adulthood for reasons that are disputed but aren't relevant to this book. As an empirical matter, the onset of puberty marks the point at which the size of the difference has stabilized.

The tests that meet these criteria are standardizations of the major IQ tests, large federally sponsored studies using cognitive test batteries with good measures of $g$ ("$g$-loaded," in the jargon) and the longitudinal assessments of academic achievement known as the National Assessment of Educational Progress (NAEP, pronounced "nape").[6] I summarize those studies with scatterplots. The online documentation contains downloadable Excel tables with all the data used to create them.

### *IQ Standardization Samples*

When a new edition of an IQ test has been developed, has met the appropriate psychometric standards, and is ready for public use, it is standardized on a sample that can be treated as representative of the national population so that scores can be "normed" to the familiar IQ metric based on a mean of 100. The IQ standardizations that have reported results by race (some have not) are those for the Wechsler Adult Intelligence Scale, the Wechsler Intelligence Scale for Children, the Stanford-Binet Intelligence Scales, the Woodcock-Johnson Tests of Cognitive Abilities, and the Kaufman Adolescent/Adult Intelligence Scale.

The strength of the IQ standardization samples is that they represent the best available measures of cognitive ability. If you have reason to evaluate your own profile of mental abilities or that of your child, your best choice by far is one of the major IQ tests individually administered by someone who has been trained for that job. The disadvantage of the standardization samples is that the subsamples of Africans, Latins, and Asians are often small – a few hundred people – and small samples usually mean less reliable group results. Small samples also make subgroup results sensitive to even minor divergences from the sample stratification strategy.

## Large Federally Sponsored Studies
## Using g-Loaded Test Batteries

I have already mentioned Project Talent from 1960 and the Equal Educational Opportunity Survey from 1965, which resulted in the Coleman Report. (NB: A year in this discussion always refers to the year in which the cognitive tests were administered, not the year when results were published.) Both studies used test batteries explicitly designed to measure *g*, and both indicated a European–African difference exceeding 15 IQ points, but they are the only nationally representative results of any kind available for the entire decade, so the scatterplots that follow start at 1970.

The two most important of the federally sponsored studies are the National Longitudinal Survey of Youth started in 1979 and the one started in 1997, which are among the most widely used American social science databases. The cognitive tests they employed were administered in 1980 and 1998 respectively. Both studies used the Armed Forces Qualification Test (AFQT), a highly *g*-loaded test battery.

In 1972, the National Center for Education Statistics launched the first in a series of nationally representative longitudinal studies: the National Longitudinal Study of the High School Class of 1972. It was followed by High School and Beyond in 1980 (I use two cohorts from that study, one tested in 1980 and the other tested in 1982), the National Education Longitudinal Study of 1988, the Education Longitudinal Study of 2002, and the High School Longitudinal Study of 2009. The 1988 and 2002 studies used only tests of reading and mathematics and are classified with NAEP as achievement tests. The 2009 study administered only a mathematics test and does not qualify for the inventory.

### The National Assessment of Educational Progress

NAEP is a congressionally mandated program administered by the National Center for Education Statistics. It periodically tests large and nationally representative samples of students in the fourth, eighth, and twelfth grades. NAEP's purpose is to measure educational achievement. It has occasionally administered other tests on subjects such as science and civics, but the core NAEP examinations consist of a reading test and a math test.

Despite its stated goal of measuring academic achievement, the NAEP reading and math tests are inevitably correlated with $g$, as are all academic achievement tests.[7] However, academic achievement tests are less complete measures of $g$ than IQ tests. There's more to cognitive ability than reading and math; add in highly $g$-loaded tests of related but distinct abilities, and the differences between groups that are revealed are likely to become larger.[8] The implication is that race differences on the NAEP tests, the NELS-88, and the ELS-2002 are probably smaller than they would have been if an IQ-like test battery had been administered.

Furthermore, NAEP does not administer both math and reading tests to the same students, so the two scores cannot be combined into a composite score, as is done in the other studies. Rather than engage in the statistical assumptions that would have been necessary to combine the NAEP reading and math scores, I computed the race differences using the known means and standard deviations (see below) for the reading and math scores separately and then used the mean of those two differences to represent the race difference. Using the mean of the two scores tends to underestimate the difference (as explained in the note).[9]

One other wrinkle of the NAEP scores is that the National Center for Education Statistics sponsors two series of tests: the regular NAEP tests, which may be modified from year to year to reflect developments in the high school curriculum, and the tests administered as part of the Long-Term Trend Assessment program, designed to be consistent over time. Every NAEP test, whether part of the standard administrations or the Long-Term Trend Assessment, consists of a large, nationally representative, stand-alone sample using technically excellent tests of math and reading. If no other issues were involved, I would have included all of the administrations in the analysis, but some had to be omitted for reasons explained in the online documentation.

*Interpreting the Scores*

In the pages to come, I refer to cognitive tests that use different scoring systems. There's a way to compare them using means and standard deviations to create what are known as *standard scores* or *z-scores*. They're useful once you become familiar with them, but most readers are more likely to be familiar with IQ scores, so I will use the IQ metric to describe cognitive ability whenever I'm describing means taken from a nationally representative sample. In Chapter 5, when I'm dealing with the unrepresentative samples of students who self-select to take admissions tests for college and professional schools – the SAT, ACT, GRE, MCAT, and LSAT – I use standardized scores.

When I refer to mean differences among races, I express the difference in terms of *standard deviations*, with the abbreviation *SD*. If that term is new to you, the note gives you a primer.[10] Here are the basics:

> A standard deviation is a measure of how spread out a set of scores is – in essence, it is the typical difference between the individual numbers in a set and the mean for that set.

> *z*-scores are normed to have a mean of zero and a standard deviation of 1.

> IQ scores are normed to have a population mean of 100 and a standard deviation of 15.

*Normed* means that the raw scores are converted to fit a predetermined mean and standard deviation. This kind of conversion can be done legitimately with any trait that is distributed normally – meaning that the distribution of raw scores approximates a bell curve.[11]

As a rough guide to interpreting sizes of differences, think of a difference of half an SD as "moderate" and a difference of one SD as "large." To give you some concrete examples:

If you have an IQ of 100, you are at the mean of the U.S. national population – the 50th percentile. Doing well in high school is not a problem, and you can flourish in a wide variety of postsecondary technical training programs or get an AA degree. But getting a BA in a traditional liberal arts major is challenging, and a BS in a STEM major (science, technology, engineering, mathematics) is probably not in the cards.

If you have an IQ of 115 – one SD above the mean – you are at the 84th percentile of the national population. You can successfully get a degree in most college majors, though maybe not as a STEM major at a tough school.

If you have an IQ of 130, two SDs above the mean, you are in the 98th percentile. You meet a common definition of *gifted*.

If you have an IQ of 145, three SDs above the mean,

you are in the top tenth of the top percentile and can probably get a PhD in any discipline that attracts you. If you have reasonable interpersonal skills to go with your cognitive ability, you will be avidly courted by employers. If your skills tilt toward math or programming, many hedge funds and Silicon Valley companies will be indifferent to your interpersonal skills – they'll offer you riches regardless.

Expressing comparisons in terms of percentiles can be useful, which is why I sometimes report them. But when the objective is to express differences between groups, percentiles can be misleading because the effective "width" of a percentile becomes greater as it gets further from the mean. For example, two students at the 43rd and 56th percentiles of cognitive ability are 13 percentiles apart and about 5 IQ points apart, a difference of 0.33 SDs. Substantively, the difference in cognitive ability between the two students is so small that even the most perceptive teachers cannot easily guess which student has which score.

Now consider two students at the 86.9th and 99.9th percentiles. They too are exactly 13 percentiles apart. But their respective IQs are 117 and 146, a difference of 1.93 SDs. Unless there is a misleading personality factor, a perceptive teacher will know without doubt which student has which score after the first day. Perhaps after the first fifteen minutes.

If you're not convinced, here's another example. A score that puts someone at the 99th percentile is obviously high, and it is natural to think it doesn't make a lot of difference to get more precise. But that's illusory. Every starter on every men's basketball team for every major university in the country is probably in the 99th percentile on a scale of male basketball ability – but that's the same percentile that LeBron James is in. Percentiles are grossly inadequate for conveying differences in performance at the high end.

## THE DIFFERENCES

This section summarizes the results from the assembled inventory of mental test scores, comparing the European means with the African, Latin, and Asian means. I use scatterplots to show you how the differences have changed from 1970 to 2019.

The scatterplots use unadorned data, giving you a picture of what happens when race differences in scores from all of the relevant studies are thrown into the pot. When the data are examined analytically, more complicated stories emerge – but those more complicated stories are themselves subject to alternative interpretations. The online documentation provides interested readers with downloadable files containing all the data used to prepare the scatterplots and associated data that enable more complicated analyses. I discuss them in the online documentation.

### *The European–African Difference*

The race difference in cognitive ability that has caused by far the most controversy and angst since the 1960s is the difference between America's Africans and Europeans. It also is informed by the most data – fifty-nine estimates, adding up the age breakdowns from the studies in my inventory. The figure below shows how the size of the difference varied from 1972 to 2019.

The solid black circles in the plot indicate results from the average of math and reading tests (all but two are from NAEP), while the white circles indicate IQ standardizations or *g*-loaded tests in federal surveys.

The figure shows a major reduction in the difference during the 1970s and into the 1980s. Exactly when the narrowing stopped is open to interpretation. Regression

European–African Difference in Mental Test Scores
Expressed in Standard Deviations

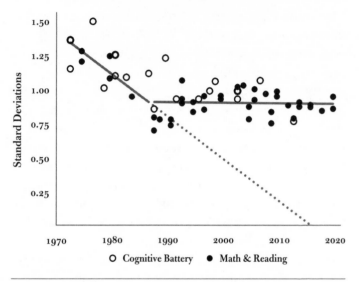

analyses show that the trendline was nearly flat for tests conducted from 1983 through 2019. But 1987 saw the lowest mean for any year (0.69 SDs), so I will use 1987 to illustrate the change in the trendlines.

Suppose you had been analyzing these data near the end of the 1980s and had all the information in the graph through 1987. Looking at the graph, you can visualize a line that characterizes the downward slant of the European–African difference from 1972 to 1987. The statistically "best" possible straight line is one that minimizes the error over the whole set of observations even though the line seldom passes through the exact value of any given observation. The best line for the European–African difference is represented by the downward-sloping gray line. Its values for 1972 and 1987 are 1.33 SDs and 0.87 SDs respectively, representing a reduction of a third from the 1972 difference. You would have had excellent reason for optimism. As the dotted extension of the line shows, the European–African gap in test scores would have gone to zero by 2015 if that trend had continued. But it did not. The nearly flat gray line represents the trend from 1987 through 2019.

A more optimistic story emerges when the test results are analyzed separately by program. For example, both sets of NAEP administrations show a declining European–African difference from the late 1990s through the most recent administrations. On the other hand, the NAEP reductions come after the increases in the early 1990s, so the net differences are larger for both eighth-graders and twelfth-graders than they were at their low point in the late 1980s.

I hope to deflect potential debates about trends over time by using an estimate of the current difference that is conservative in two respects. First, the estimate is based on tests administered from 2010 to 2019, when European–African differences have been at their smallest since the late 1980s. Second, nine of the ten tests during that period are academic achievement tests – meaning that nine of ten measures tend to understate differences in $g$ that would be revealed by full-scale cognitive test batteries. The mean of the ten measures of the European–African estimate works out to 0.85 SDs.

### The European–Latin Difference

The European–Latin difference in mental test scores is consistently smaller than the European–African difference, but it remains substantial.

I have drawn a linear trendline to help organize your view of the history, but obviously the story is more complicated than that – notably, the difference increased during the 1990s, then resumed its decline in the early 2000s.

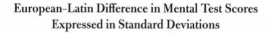

European–Latin Difference in Mental Test Scores
Expressed in Standard Deviations

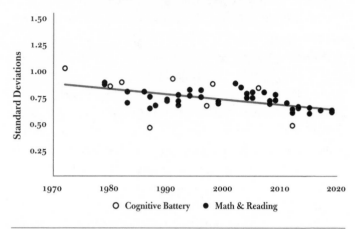

The fitted values for the European–Latin difference in 1972 and 2019 are 0.87 SDs and 0.63 SDs respectively – a reduction of 28 percent. The decline shows no signs of ending. I have no satisfactory explanation for the rise in the difference during the 1990s. A close examination of changes in the nature of the Latin immigrant pool over that period might give some clues.

The mean difference in the eleven test results during the 2010s is 0.62 SDs, and that will serve as my estimate of the current European–Latin difference.

### *The European–Asian Difference*

When Richard Herrnstein and I were writing *The Bell Curve* in the early 1990s, our assessment was that Asians had a higher mean IQ than Europeans, but the fragmentary data then available made that conclusion quite tentative. By now the evidence has piled up and is conclusive. On average, Asians outscore Europeans, Africans, and Latins.

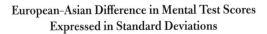

European–Asian Difference in Mental Test Scores
Expressed in Standard Deviations

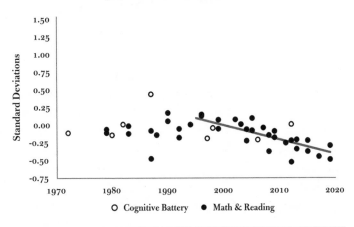

This graph has something new: negative values on the vertical axis, which are needed to show when Asians have a higher mean test score than Europeans. The farther below zero, the larger the Asian advantage.

The generally small but irregular European–Asian difference into the 1990s is typical of the spread of results when sample sizes are small, as they were for some of those tests. But a more important explanation, albeit speculative, is that large-scale Asian immigration began in the 1970s with large numbers of Vietnamese refugees whose children were still being acculturated to America and used English as their second language when they took the NAEP in the 1980s. Subsequent Asian immigration has drawn heavily from highly educated East Asians and South Asians. The more consistent results from the mid-1990s onward could reflect a more consistently talented immigrant pool.

The trendline is based on 1995–2019, when the fitted values of the European–Asian difference went from 0.09 SDs to −0.39 SDs, a remarkable net change of nearly half a standard deviation in twenty-four years. The estimate of the current European–Asian difference, like the others, uses tests from the 2010s, which averaged –0.30 SDs.

### Estimates of the Current Differences

Using tests administered during the 2010s, which in effect means NAEP, the mean European–African difference was 0.85 SDs, the mean European–Latin difference was 0.62 SDs, and the mean European–Asian difference was –0.30 SDs. Assuming a mean of 100 and SD of 15 for IQ, the corresponding equivalents in IQ points are 12.75, 9.30, and 4.50 respectively.

My estimate of European IQ is the mean of the four IQ standardizations from the 2000s, which works out to 103.35. Thus we are left with mean IQ estimates of 90.60 for Africans, 94.05 for Latins, and 107.85 for Asians.

Rounding estimated IQ to the nearest whole number, here are the means and their percentiles in the national distribution that I will use for the rest of the book:

|          | Estimated Mean IQ | z-score Equivalent | Percentile Equivalent |
|----------|-------------------|--------------------|-----------------------|
| European | 103               | 0.20               | 58                    |
| African  | 91                | –0.60              | 27                    |
| Latin    | 94                | –0.40              | 34                    |
| Asian    | 108               | 0.53               | 70                    |

For all three minorities, we should expect that disaggregation into subgroups would produce different estimates. It would be useful to have separate measures for Africans who remained in the rural South, recent African immigrants, and all other Africans; separate measures for European Latins, Mestizo Latins, and indigenous Latins; and separate measures for East Asians, Southeast Asians, and South Asians. But the data for making good estimates don't exist.[12]

What do these estimates of current race differences mean for daily life where you live? Probably not much. Maybe you work in a big city where the means are reasonably close to those in the table above, while the means in the suburb where you live are radically different. Maybe you live in a small town with only a few minority families. They have no significant group mean – they are just individuals. Maybe you live in a college town where the means around campus are very different from those in the surrounding community.

The information about race differences in mean cognitive ability is useful only as background information for thinking about issues at a societal level. The figure below shows the distributions of cognitive ability for the four races from two perspectives.

The top figure shows how much overlap exists in the distributions. It is not a threatening picture. Yes, differences exist, but it is also true that millions of Africans and Latins have higher cognitive ability than millions of Europeans and Asians. The top figure should also serve as an object lesson in the necessity of judging people as individuals, not members of groups. If you rely on the difference in means you are going to make a huge number of mistakes about individuals.

The bottom figure shows why race differences in cognitive ability nonetheless have consequences for the society as a whole. The differences in the raw numbers of individuals on the right-hand side of the bell curve become larger as IQ goes up. Among people of the four races with IQs of 100, 70 percent are European or Asian. For IQs of 115, 85 percent. For IQs of 125, 90 percent. For IQs of 140, 96 percent.

Since the most prestigious, powerful, and highest paying jobs are so concentrated among people on the right-hand

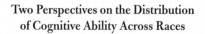

Two Perspectives on the Distribution
of Cognitive Ability Across Races

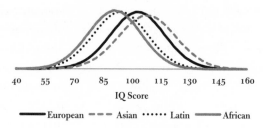

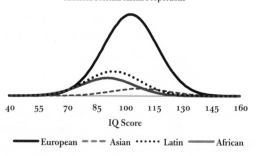

side of the distribution, a variety of important social and economic consequences are not just possible. They are inevitable. Chapter 5 takes up a few of the most important ones.

## Are Race Differences in Test Scores Meaningful?

It is time to confront the issue that will have led many readers to discount everything that has come before in this chapter. How can we expect that an African or Latin child growing up in poverty, going to terrible schools, and victimized by systemic racism will score well on tests designed by White people to measure things that White people have decided are important?

That reaction and its variations often conflate two positions. The first is the one I held when I was writing *Losing Ground*, which was that meaningful differences exist but we know how to shrink them. It's just a matter of implementing solutions that will make the remaining differences too small to worry about. The other position, and one that I'm sure many readers hold, is that the tests don't measure African and Latin cognitive ability accurately. They are biased in favor of Europeans and Asians and biased against Africans and Latins.

*"We know how to fix it."* Regarding the first position, that improved education (especially early education) will reduce race differences, I could lay out what we know about the malleability of cognitive ability, the record on interventions intended to raise cognitive ability, and the persistence of race differences in mean test scores even among children from socioeconomically privileged families. I have written about such issues at length elsewhere.[13] The short story is that ordinary exposure to education does indeed have an effect on cognitive ability for all children, but that no one has yet found a way to increase cognitive ability permanently over and above the effects of routine education. The success stories consist of modest effects on exit tests that fade out. Most experimental programs don't achieve even that much. We know how to improve education for children at every cognitive level, but we don't know how to change their cognitive levels.

The NAEP results give us a simpler way to think about the intractability of the problem. The mean differences separating European teenagers from African teenagers in math and reading haven't diminished since the last half of the 1980s. That's more than three decades during which hundreds of billions of dollars have been poured into attempts to improve the education of disadvantaged children, including the intense effort to reduce test-score differences through No Child Left Behind. To dismiss the differences in mean test scores that I have described as a problem that we know how to fix if we try hard enough is a triumph of hope over a very great deal of experience.

*"The tests are biased."* Now we come to a position that is taken for granted by much of the public but has nearly disappeared in technical literature of this century because there are so few unresolved questions.

The accusations of test bias take many forms. The most common is probably the assumption that a person from a poor and marginalized community won't be able to answer many of the questions because the answers depend on knowledge or vocabulary to which they have not been exposed. Other issues include whether African and Latin youngsters are as motivated to perform well on tests and the assumption that test scores are sensitive to the amount of test prep that a student gets. Perhaps the tests don't measure the same construct in people of different races – for example, an IQ test might measure cognitive ability in Europeans, but it's actually measuring socioeconomic status in Africans.

All of these possibilities have been investigated minutely. But all of them are ancillary to the central practical question about bias in mental tests: Do the test results underpredict the performance of minorities in real-life situations?

Tests of cognitive ability have value because they help in predicting things that people want to know about. Admissions committees for college want to know how an applicant is likely to do in college. Employers want to know how well an applicant is likely to perform on the job. Whatever the combination of sources of test bias might be, genuine bias against a minority will show up in a way that leaves no room for doubt: It will underpredict the test taker's performance in the classroom or on the job.

Whether predictive validity is the same for different groups can be subjected to rigorous statistical scrutiny, and it has been, repeatedly.[14] The results are unambiguous, whether the thing being predicted is grades in school or performance on the job. *The major tests do not underpredict the performance of Africans or Latins.*

Just because a test doesn't underpredict minority performance doesn't exclude the possibility of other problems. Suppose, for example, that the test *over*predicts African classroom performance – a phenomenon that has often been found for tests of academic aptitude. In such cases, the SAT or ACT scores predict that Africans will have better grades and graduation rates than they actually achieve. This could be explained by everything from cultural differences in ways that students approach homework to racist teachers giving African students low marks, but none of the potential explanations support the proposition that the test is biased *against* Africans.

You may still be unsatisfied. The statistical evidence doesn't lend itself to straightforward tables or graphs. I can, however, give you some concrete evidence of how solid the professional consensus is.

In 1995, in the wake of the controversy over *The Bell Curve*, the American Psychological Association established a task force of eleven of the nation's most eminent scholars of cognitive ability. They represented a wide range of theoretical perspectives – the disagreements that those eleven had among themselves about cognitive ability and testing were many and deep. Their assignment was to prepare a summary of the state of knowledge regarding the measurement of intelligence that all of them could agree on. They did so, unanimously signing off on their report, with no minority dissents. The following is the entirety of what the task force wrote about test bias:

It is often argued that the lower mean scores of African Americans reflect a bias in the intelligence tests themselves. This argument is right in one sense of "bias" but wrong in another. To see the first of these, consider how the term is used in probability theory. When a coin comes up heads consistently for any reason it is said to be "biased," regardless of any consequences that the outcome may or may not have. In this sense the Black/White score differential is ipso facto evidence of what may be called "outcome bias." African Americans are subject to outcome bias not only with respect to tests but along many dimensions of American life. They have the short end of nearly every stick: average income, representation in high-level occupations, health and health care, death rate, confrontations with the legal system, and so on. With this situation in mind, some critics regard the test score differential as just another example of a pervasive outcome bias that characterizes our society as a whole. Although there is a sense in which they are right, this critique ignores the particular social purpose that tests are designed to serve.

From an educational point of view, the chief function of mental tests is as predictors. Intelligence tests predict school performance fairly well, at least in American schools as they are now constituted. Similarly, achievement tests are fairly good predictors of performance in college and postgraduate settings. Considered in this light, the relevant question is whether the tests have a "predictive bias" against Blacks. Such a bias would exist if African-American performance on the criterion variables (school achievement, college GPA, etc.) were systematically higher than the same subjects' test scores would predict. This is not the case. The actual regression lines (which show the mean criterion performance for individuals who got various scores on the predictor) for Blacks do not lie above those for Whites; there is even a slight tendency in the other direction. Considered as predictors of future performance, the tests do not seem to be biased against African Americans.

The language of testing is a standard form of English with which some Blacks may not be familiar; specific vocabulary items are often unfamiliar to Black children; the tests are often given by White examiners rather than by more familiar Black teachers; African Americans may not be motivated to work hard on tests that so clearly reflect White values; the time demands of some tests may be alien to Black culture. (Similar suggestions have been made in connection with the test performance of Hispanic Americans.) Many of these suggestions are plausible, and such mechanisms may play a role in particular cases. Controlled studies have shown, however, that none of them contributes substantially to the Black/White differential under discussion here.

Nothing in the literature in the twenty-six years since the task force issued its report has successfully challenged these findings.

If this is still too obscure to be persuasive, there's an easier way to think about whether tests are biased against Africans and Latins. It's not just psychometricians who analyze these things. All the top colleges have quantified expectations of the students that they accept. They keep track of how students perform relative to those expectations. If any of these colleges had any evidence whatsoever that their African or Latin students outperform the expectations

based on their SAT or ACT scores, they would have pub-
licized it in every way possible as evidence of excellence in
educating minorities.

You may know inspiring true stories about individual
African or Latin students who have done well in college
despite disadvantages they had to overcome, but you won't
have seen such stories about African or Latin students as a
group. Many African and Latin students are admitted to
selective colleges with low test scores. College administrators would be ecstatic if those low scores turned out to be
illusory for those students as a group. They aren't. That's
what lies behind the bloodless finding in the technical literature that the predictive validity of test scores is the same
for different races. If it weren't true, you would have heard
about it long ago.

The movement to get colleges to stop using the SAT,
ACT, and GRE is gaining ground. There are serious arguments for dropping the tests that don't rely on accusations
of test bias. My own view is that the goals of the SAT could
be met with achievement tests that don't carry the controversies associated with test bias and the rumored magic of
test prep. To prepare for an achievement test in chemistry,
you don't need to learn test-taking tricks. You just need to
study chemistry. Such arguments are not driving the movement to get rid of the tests, however. The activists say that
the tests are worthless – products of White privilege,
designed to perpetuate White privilege. In their minds,
they don't need evidence of bias; the *existence* of lower
mean scores for Africans and Latins is in itself irrefutable
evidence of bias because everyone knows there are no race
differences in intelligence. This is argued with all the pas-
sion and conviction that true believers bring to their evan-
gelism. It does not reflect reality.

# Race Differences in Violent Crime

MURDER, RAPE, ROBBERY, and physical assault are crimes everywhere. Theft is a crime everywhere. By that core definition of *crime*, only a small minority of people in any race in any nation are criminals. Every race has such a minority and also a subset of that minority who are chronically criminal. But the sizes of these minorities are different among America's Europeans, Africans, Latins, and Asians, and they have produced large differences in crime rates.

Causes are as irrelevant to the purposes of this chapter as they were to the discussion of cognitive ability. Thus I do not discuss the legacy of slavery, the effects of poverty or absent fathers, the genetic etiology of criminality, or why crime rates rise and fall over time. These are all potentially important. They have also been the subjects of longstanding and unresolved scholarly debates. My point is that the existence of large race differences in crime rates is a fact, and one that has sweeping social consequences.

This chapter is exclusively about the most serious crimes, called *index offenses* by the FBI – the ones used to create the violent crime index and property crime index included in the annual report, *Crime in the United States*, a product of the FBI's Uniform Crime Reporting (UCR) program. The offenses in the violent crime index are murder, rape, robbery, and aggravated assault ("aggravated"

47

meaning that the assault involved a serious injury, plausible threat of serious injury, or use of a deadly weapon). The offenses that make up the property crime index are burglary, larceny, motor vehicle theft, and arson.

My focus, here and in Chapter 6, is on violent crime. The fear of being raped, robbed, beaten up, or killed is visceral in a way that doesn't apply to the threat of burglary or having your car stolen. Violent crime is also hard to prevent. The most common form of robbery is the street mugging, a threat that individuals can manage only by constant awareness and defensive precautions while walking a city street – and even those measures often aren't enough. The same is true of the threats of rape and aggravated assault. The best way to avoid becoming a victim of violent crime is to stay away from the parts of town where the violent crime is concentrated at the times of day when the most crime is committed – if you're affluent enough not to live in those parts of town. If you do live in those parts of town, there's no escape.

## Arrests for Violent Crime in Thirteen Cities

The social scientist's view of who commits crimes is a set of snapshots – the report of a crime, an arrest, the decision to prosecute, the charge on which the suspect is tried, the outcome of the prosecution, and the sentence for a guilty plea or verdict. At each step, the authorities are usually trying to get it right, but "getting it right" means different things. Decisions to prosecute depend on many factors besides the likelihood that the arrested person committed the crime (e.g., whether there is evidence to prove guilt beyond reasonable doubt if it goes to trial). The decision about the charges that will be filed is a main bargaining chip in a plea bargain negotiation. A prosecution can succeed or fail for reasons having nothing to do with guilt (e.g., evidence thrown out for procedural reasons). A sentence can be affected by mitigating circumstances, the offender's age, or other factors that are independent of the nature of the crime.

Of the alternatives for measuring differences in crime, the best is arrest rates for the most serious crimes.[1] It comes down to this: Police make mistakes in arresting people, but in a well-run police department those mistakes are like measurement error in other social science topics – sufficiently random that it doesn't materially affect the results in large samples.

But can we assume that police departments are well run? One of the major contentions of those who say America is systemically racist is that police behavior is corrupted by racism. After presenting the arrest data, I therefore turn to triangulating measures to assess whether arrests accurately reflect criminal behavior.

The FBI reports national totals of arrests by race and it reports arrests by city, but the FBI does not report arrests by race for cities. This poses a major problem in comparing arrest rates by race. Differences at the national level are substantially understated, for reasons explained in the note.[2] Until recently, no major police department had released data on arrests by race. During the last few years, however, the Open Data movement, a combination of governmental and private initiatives, has assisted governments at the state, county, and city levels in creating publicly accessible databases. Many police departments have participated. Usually the police department's Open Data portal consists of some summary statistics or maps of recent criminal activity, but some cities have posted comprehensive databases, often going back several years, that include information about every arrest. Most of those databases do not disclose the race of the person arrested, but some do. I found thirteen police departments that have posted downloadable databases of arrests by race.[3] They include three of the largest cities in the country – New York City, Los Angeles, and Chicago – plus the nation's capital, Washington, D.C. The remaining nine cities offer a mix of sizes, with populations ranging from 621,849 (Baltimore) to just 42,375 (Urbana, Illinois).

The thirteen cities are scattered around the country. The Northeast is represented by New York City and the West Coast by Los Angeles. Two of the cities are in the Mid-Atlantic (Baltimore and Washington), four are in the South (Asheville, Charleston, Fayetteville, and Fort Lauderdale), three are in the Midwest (Chicago, Lincoln, and Urbana), and two are in the Southwest (Tucson and Chandler, Arizona). The African populations in the thirteen cities range from 4 percent (Lincoln) to 62 percent (Baltimore). The Latin populations range from 5 percent (Baltimore) to 48 percent (Los Angeles).

The measure of interest here is the racial ratio of arrests for violent crimes, focusing on two comparisons: the number of African arrests per 100,000 people divided by the number of European arrests per 100,000, and the number of Latin arrests per 100,000 divided by the number of European arrests per 100,000. In all the ratios I present, the larger number is divided by the smaller, so the denominator is always 1. To simplify the presentation, I will report just the numerator. For example, a ratio of 2.5 to 1 will be expressed as a ratio of 2.5. Table 2 below shows the African/European and Latin/European ratios for the combined violent crimes. A separate table for murder follows presently.

Table 2 omits ratios involving Asians because very low Asian crime rates yielded absurdly large ratios in most of the

*Table 2*
*Ratios of Violent Arrest Rates in Thirteen Cities*

| City | Years | Population in 000s | African/ European Ratio | Latin/ European Ratio |
|------|-------|--------------------|-------------------------|-----------------------|
| New York NY | 2006–2019 | 8,375 | 11.6 | 4.1 |
| Los Angeles CA | 2010–2019 | 3,921 | 9.0 | 2.4 |
| Chicago IL | 2014–2017 | 2,714 | 14.5 | 2.8 |
| Washington DC | 2013–2019 | 682 | 19.9 | 6.4 |
| Baltimore MD | 2014–2019 | 610 | 5.3 | |
| Tucson AZ | 2011–2019 | 533 | 5.5 | 1.6 |
| Lincoln NE | 2013–2018 | 279 | 13.3 | 1.7 |
| Chandler AZ | 2013–2019 | 256 | 5.7 | 2.5 |
| Fayetteville NC | 2010–2019 | 205 | 4.0 | |
| Fort Lauderdale | 2015–2019 | 180 | 9.0 | 1.3 |
| Charleston SC | 2015–2019 | 139 | 10.2 | |
| Asheville NC | 2012–2019 | 90 | 5.2 | |
| Urbana IL | 1988–2014 | 37 | 11.3 | 1.2 |
| Median | | | 9.0 | 2.4 |
| Mean | | | 9.6 | 2.7 |
| Mean weighted by population | | | 11.2 | 3.2 |

Note: Latins were not broken out as a racial category in the databases for Asheville, Baltimore, Charleston, and Fayetteville.[4] Population represents the city's mean over the years covered by the arrest data.

thirteen cities. For example, Fort Lauderdale recorded just one arrest of an Asian for a violent offense from 2015 through 2019 among the 3,000 Asians who lived there during that period. But Asian arrest rates were exceptionally low even in most cities with large Asian populations. The lone exception to the rule was New York, where the Asian violent crime rate was marginally higher than the European one.

The African/European ratios in Table 2 are extremely large. The median African/European ratio was 9.0, the simple mean was 9.6, and the mean weighted by population was 11.2. In the three megalopolises – New York, Los Angeles, and Chicago – the ratios were 11.6, 9.0, and 14.5 respectively. In the nation's capital, the ratio was 19.9.

The Latin/European ratios were smaller than the African/European ratios, but usually big enough to be significant, with a weighted mean of 3.2 across all thirteen cities. As in the case of the African ratios, the Latin ratios were biggest in the largest and most important cities. In New York, Los Angeles, Chicago, and Washington, the ratios were 4.1, 2.4, 2.9, and 6.3 respectively. The Latin/European ratios look small only by comparison with the African/European ratios. If the arrest data accurately represent race differences in violent offenses, Table 2 makes the point of this chapter.

## TRIANGULATING MEASURES

That "if" raises the key question. Can race differences in arrest rates be interpreted as race differences in criminal behavior, or is it plausible that instead they reflect racism that leads the police to arrest Africans (and, to a lesser extent, Latins) on flimsy or concocted evidence? There is a technical literature about this question, summarized in the note, that supports the validity of arrest rates.[5] For example, here's the conclusion of the largest and most rigorous study, which examined 335,619 incidents of violent crime in which the victim saw the offender: "Multivariate logistic regression results show the odds of arrest for white offenders is approximately 22% higher for robbery, 13% higher for aggravated assault, and 9% higher for simple assault than they are for black offenders." This amounts to strong evidence that arrest statistics are not biased against Africans, but it's not what one would call a transparent analysis. I can offer two statistically less powerful but more understandable ways of triangulating the arrest data.

*Arrests for Murder*

As social science data points, arrests for index offenses are not created equal. Rape and aggravated assault have gray areas that can make it difficult to be sure that the criminal offense actually occurred and, if it did, whether it meets the threshold for an index offense instead of a lesser offense. Robbery is more clear-cut – the definition requires that property be taken directly from the victim – but the most common form of robbery is a street mugging in which the victim is not injured. Such muggings are too numerous and too hard to solve for the police to devote significant resources to each one.

An arrest for murder has considerable credibility as a data point. Something serious definitely happened (there's a corpse). And while mysterious deaths are a staple of detective fiction, homicides for which there's any doubt that a crime was committed are a small proportion of the total.

An arrest for murder also carries more weight than arrests for less serious crimes because it is likely to reflect more careful police scrutiny. For most kinds of crime, the decision to arrest leaves much to the police officer's judgment, and this makes it hard to test allegations that police apply a less demanding threshold for arresting Africans and Latins than they do for Europeans. An arrest for murder is insulated from that charge not just by the integrity of individual police officers, but by the special attention that police departments everywhere devote to the most serious crimes. Homicide is at the top of the list. In large cities, homicides and attempted homicides are often investigated by a special unit composed of the force's top-rated detectives.

Smaller police departments faced with a homicide routinely call in specialized help from county or state agencies. I don't think it is idealistic to conclude that an arrest for murder is typically the result of a serious investigation conducted by people who know what they're doing. If arrests for murder show the same (or greater) race differences as arrests for the other offenses, there is reason to think that real differences in criminality explain them.

Perhaps you think I'm too trusting of the police. Let's go to the opposite extreme, then, and assume the worst: that police racism is rampant. I ask you to think in terms of statistics rather than the many vivid and outrageous specific examples of injustice that can be cited, and – this is hard to do – ignore whether the police arrested the right person. The only question on the table is whether the statistics on the race of the people arrested for murder accurately reflect the race of the perpetrators.

For homicides nationwide from 2010 through 2019, 76 percent of alleged perpetrators knew the victim, as a family member or an acquaintance. Virtually all of those homicides were what criminologists call "expressive" murders: the result of arguments, brawls, jealousy, and other interpersonal conflicts. An extremely high proportion of the alleged perpetrators of these crimes were in fact guilty – expressive murders are usually impulsive and occur without precautions against getting caught; they are often witnessed; and the forensic evidence is often abundant.

Here's where we need to think in purely statistical terms. Consider the combination of de facto residential segregation and racial self-segregation in circles of friends, spouses, lovers, and acquaintances. This means that in cases where perpetrator and victim were part of the same family or were personally acquainted, the race of the person arrested was likely to be the same as the race of the actual perpetrator even when the police made a mistake.

Now let's look at the 24 percent of homicides in which the victim was a stranger to the arrested suspect. About 13 percent of all murders are gang-related. Gangs are almost always restricted to a single race. If an African is killed in gang-related violence between an African gang and a Latin gang, the chances that the culprit is Latin is exceedingly high – and vice versa. Almost all the people arrested for gang-related murders are likely to be of the same race as the perpetrator, even if the wrong individuals are arrested in some cases. At the same time, a high proportion of gang-related murders involve strangers. I don't have the data to be more specific, but a great many of the 24 percent of homicides that involve strangers also involve perpetrators whose race can be accurately guessed just by knowing what gangs are involved.

At this point, we're reduced to a small set of murders in which racist police could deform the statistics on the race of offenders: murders in which the perpetrator did not know the victim, that were not gang-related, and in which the person identified as the offender was an African. That set amounted to about 4 percent of all homicides from 2010 to 2019. You can think the worst of the police, and point to cases where the person arrested was later found innocent, and still you would have to accept that the aggregate statistics on the race of perpetrators of murders are reasonably accurate.

Table 3 below shows the ratios for murder arrests for all thirteen cities in our analysis. Recall that Latin arrest rates were not available for Asheville, Baltimore, Charleston, or Fayetteville. The Latin/European entry for Fort Lauderdale is empty because no Latin was arrested for murder in that city during the five years covered by the arrest data.

The italicized ratios in the table indicate that the denominator (the European rate) is based on a sample of six or fewer murder arrests over the entire period covered

Table 3
Arrest Rates for Murder in Thirteen Cities

| City | African/European Ratio | Latin/European Ratio |
|------|------------------------|----------------------|
| New York NY | 18.1 | 5.5 |
| Los Angeles CA | 19.8 | 5.4 |
| Chicago IL | 21.6 | 3.9 |
| Washington DC | 84.9 | 10.4 |
| Baltimore MD | 6.3 | |
| Tucson AZ | 7.2 | 1.3 |
| Lincoln NE | 33.3 | 3.7 |
| Chandler AZ | 14.1 | 7.7 |
| Fayetteville NC | 8.7 | |
| Fort Lauderdale FL | 5.5 | |
| Charleston SC | 61.4 | |
| Asheville NC | 7.4 | |
| Urbana IL | 20.3 | 2.6 |
| Median | 18.1 | 4.7 |
| Mean | 23.7 | 5.1 |
| Mean weighted by population | 21.0 | 4.9 |

by the database. In those cases, the ratio should simply be interpreted as "large" without attaching much importance to the specific number. The denominators for the rest of the cities were at least eleven murder arrests.

The African/European ratios for murder arrests are larger than the ratios for overall violent crimes in all the cities with the single exception of Fort Lauderdale. So too with the Latin/European ratios with the exceptions of Fort Lauderdale and Tucson. In other words, the crime that gets the most careful police attention shows larger racial disproportions in 18 of the 21 comparisons available. This is contrary to expectations if it is thought that the police are getting away with wrongly arresting Africans and Latins for less-scrutinized crimes. In most cases, the ratios for murder arrests were not just somewhat larger than the ones for overall violent crime but substantially larger.

### Reports of Crime to the Police

The second means of triangulation is to use reported offenses for the analysis instead of arrests. Reported offenses are those brought to the attention of the police by a member of the public, either by telling an officer on the scene or by calling 911. As an indicator that a violent crime has actually been committed, reported offenses are not as good as arrests, since a substantial proportion of reported offenses turn out to be unfounded. But reported offenses are insulated from police racism insofar as police behavior and judgments have nothing to do with whether the report was made, and the police have limited discretion in deciding whether to let the report into the official record – for 911 calls, none at all.

Another advantage of reports is that identification of the perpetrator's race is given by the person who contacted the police, usually the victim. This doesn't mean that members of the public always accurately identify the race of the perpetrators (though their accuracy rate is high), but the police haven't made the judgment. If the race distribution of alleged perpetrators is consistent with the race distribution of arrests, it is another useful indication that the arrest data are conveying interpretable information.

Eight of the thirteen cities that have released arrest data have also released their datasets for reports of crime. Of these, only the New York dataset includes the race of the reported perpetrator. The African/European ratio of reported perpetrators in New York was 14.8, higher than the arrest-based ratio of 11.6. The Latin/European ratio was 3.9, fractionally lower than the arrest-based ratio of 4.1. Neither result is consistent with the hypothesis that arrest data exaggerate minority crime.

The New York dataset of reports allows us to explore whether Africans and Latins who report crimes name African or Latin perpetrators as often as Europeans and Asians do. The short answer is that African and Latin victims of crime are much *more* likely to report that the perpetrators were African or Latin than are Europeans and Asians.[6] However, this finding is vulnerable to an artifact. If the reports come from neighborhoods that are nearly all African or all Latin, of course the overwhelming proportion of alleged perpetrators will be African or Latin. At this point, we come to an especially valuable aspect of the New York dataset: We can break down the results by zip code and thereby look at the results from racially heterogeneous neighborhoods.[7]

Even in zip codes where Africans constitute less than a quarter of the population, African victims identified 79 percent of the suspects as African and 17 percent as Latin – a total of 96 percent of the suspects. In zip codes where Latins account for less than a quarter of the population, Latin victims identified 62 percent of the suspects as African and 31 percent as Latin – a total of 93 percent of suspects.

We can carry this analysis another step by limiting the zip codes to ones where Africans and Latins *combined* constitute less than half the population. The results are essentially unchanged. African victims in such zip codes identified 82 percent of the perpetrators as African and 12 percent as Latin. In the same zip codes, Latin victims identified 49 percent of the perpetrators as African and 42 percent as Latin. When the numbers for zip codes with less than 50 percent African and Latin residents combined are converted to rates per 100,000, the African/European ratio of alleged perpetrators as reported by Africans is 26.4. The Latin/European ratio of alleged perpetrators as reported by Latins is 6.7.

In the data broken down by zip code and race of victim it is impossible to see evidence that the disproportions shown in the citywide arrest statistics are misleading. The disproportions reported by minority victims are in fact larger than the ones in the arrest statistics.

### New York City's Shootings Database

New York offers yet another way to triangulate. The New York Police Department has assembled a separate dataset of all shootings from 2006 to 2017 – not simply "shots fired," but shots that struck a human being. This dataset thus includes shootings that did not result in a fatality, and it's a big number: 81 percent of the 21,626 shootings in the NYPD database were nonfatal. By combining the shootings database with the arrest database, it is possible to create another measure: the race of probable perpetrators in cases where the NYPD concluded they knew who did it but didn't have enough evidence for an arrest.

The table on the next page shows the results when we compare New York City ratios based on victims' reports of a suspect's race, arrests for violent crimes other than murder (i.e., rape, robbery, and aggravated assaults), arrests for murder, and shootings that did not result in an arrest. Once again, the arrest data are the most conservative estimate of the racial disproportions, with the single exception of Latin suspects in reported violent offenses.

The New York database of shootings is also useful as a counterweight to much of the rhetoric from the Black Lives Matter movement. Of course they matter, no matter what the race of the shooters in the New York database may be.

| Measure | African/ European Ratio | Latin/ European Ratio |
|---|---|---|
| Suspects in reported violent offenses | 14.8 | 3.9 |
| Arrests for violent crimes other than murder | 11.3 | 4.0 |
| Arrests for murder | 17.9 | 5.5 |
| Suspected perpetrators of shootings not resulting in an arrest | 48.6 | 8.7 |

That is my final point for this discussion. Many African lives have been taken by violence, but of the 1,906 African deaths in the New York shootings database for which the race of the perpetrator is known, 89 percent were killed by Africans. Ten percent were killed by Latins. Just 0.6 percent were killed by Europeans. Of the 7,858 Africans who were wounded in shootings, 90 percent were shot by Africans, 9 percent by Latins, and 0.4 percent by Europeans.

## A Quick Look at Property Crime

Violent crime has far broader social and personal consequences than property crime. Property crime is not only less viscerally threatening than violent crime; it is also more manageable. In gentrifying urban neighborhoods, decorative iron bars for windows and secure locks and doors have been standard for decades, and they usually prevent burglary. Stealing a car used to be a simple matter of hot-wiring, but most cars now have electronic starting systems and can't be stolen unless the thief has the key. In the suburbs, house-alarm systems have become hard to bypass and are often linked to armed-response private security services. Some affluent neighborhoods in suburbs now consist of gated communities. Alarm systems and surveillance cameras make it much riskier to burglarize stores or office buildings after hours. For many people, insurance takes care of most of the problem if a property crime occurs.

Nonetheless, it is useful to take a quick look at race differences in arrests for property crime. They reinforce the effects of differences in violent crime, and to some extent they interact. Table 4 below shows the numbers for our thirteen cities.

Table 4
Ratios of Property Offense Rates in
Thirteen Cities

| City | African/European Ratio | Latin/European Ratio |
|---|---|---|
| New York NY | 5.2 | 2.0 |
| Los Angeles CA | 5.9 | 1.5 |
| Chicago IL | 6.9 | 1.2 |
| Washington DC | 10.2 | 2.8 |
| Baltimore MD | 2.7 | |
| Tucson AZ | 2.5 | 0.9 |
| Lincoln NE | 7.5 | 1.4 |
| Chandler AZ | 3.9 | 1.8 |
| Fayetteville NC | 1.7 | |
| Fort Lauderdale FL | 5.4 | 1.2 |
| Charleston SC | 3.7 | |
| Asheville NC | 3.0 | |
| Urbana IL | 6.5 | 0.7 |
| Median ratio | 5.2 | 1.4 |
| Mean ratio | 5.0 | 1.5 |
| Mean ratio weighted by population | 5.6 | 1.6 |

As in the case of violent crime, Table 4 does not show ratios involving Asians and for the same reason: arrest rates of Asians for property offenses have usually been so low that ratios became absurd.

Africans and Latins are arrested for property crimes at higher rates than Europeans – modestly so for Latins, with a mean ratio of 1.5, and much more so for Africans, with a mean ratio of 5.0. These ratios are smaller than the ones for violent crime.

## THE BOTTOM LINE

Across thirteen American cities, including four of the nation's most important ones, the African arrest rate for violent crime was usually around 9 to 11 times the European rate and the Latin arrest rate for violent crime was usually around 2 to 3 times the European rate. Asian arrest rates for violent crime ranged from minuscule to small. These are huge differences. Triangulating data indicates that the arrest rates reflect, and perhaps understate, race differences in violent criminal activity.

# First-Order Effects
## of Race Differences
## in Cognitive Ability

In this chapter and the next, I limit myself to the first-order effects of race differences in cognitive ability and violent crime. By "first-order effects" I mean those that are directly related to the measured race differences and that we know without doubt are occurring.

In this chapter I present evidence that the job market hires Europeans, Africans, Latins, and Asians with markedly different cognitive ability for the same occupation. That's a first-order effect of race differences in cognitive ability. It's happening, for whatever reasons. Is it a good thing or a bad thing? That's not a question that lends itself to "without doubt" answers and is not a topic here.

I should add that this chapter could easily be extended into a long book. Cognitive ability is associated with many personality and behavioral traits. Populations that differ in cognitive ability will also differ to some degree in those traits, with wide-ranging though usually minor effects.

## Why Cognitive Ability Is Important
## in the Job Market

Many traits help explain why some people are better at their jobs than others. Personality traits such as empathy and simple agreeableness are examples. Even more important are traits such as self-discipline, conscientiousness, and persistence. In combination, such traits sometimes explain as much of the variance in job performance as cognitive ability does. IQ is not everything. Cognitive ability is nonetheless important in the workplace, and not just for a few intellectually demanding jobs. You have probably observed this for yourself.

In elementary school, you probably had good teachers who engaged with their students, getting the material across and then motivating the students to explore it. You probably also had bad teachers who became defensive and hostile when students asked questions. The difference would have been partly a matter of personality, but another reason was that some teachers were smart enough to deal with students' questions and others weren't.

You have likely noticed how some waitstaff in a crowded restaurant can cope with the hectic pace while others mix up orders and can't keep track of which tables need what and when. Part of the explanation is how smart they are: the good ones are dealing efficiently with queueing problems.

Many of you have had small children for whom you chose nannies, or elderly parents for whom you chose home-care providers. In both cases, your priorities in selecting among job candidates were probably warmth and conscientiousness, but you also undoubtedly worried about how candidates would respond to an unexpected problem. You were trying to assess how smart they were, because being "smart enough" when an unexpected problem occurs is an essential part of the job.

If you worked at menial jobs in high school or during summers while in college, you found at first hand that even the most menial jobs can be done well or poorly, efficiently or inefficiently, for reasons that involve cognitive ability.

What you have observed in your own experience with the world is common knowledge to employers. Competence matters in every occupation, and cognitive ability is part of the explanation for competence. Not surprisingly, recognition of that fact has led to an enormous amount of research about the relationship of cognitive ability to job productivity. The technical literature is so extensive that the chapter on cognitive abilities in the most recent edition of *The Oxford Handbook of Personnel Assessment and Selection* (2014) is not a meta-analysis of existing studies; it is a review of many meta-analyses.

The consistent findings about cognitive ability and job performance that apply most directly to group differences in cognitive ability are these:

> Measures of cognitive ability and job performance are always positively correlated.

> The size of the correlation goes up as the job becomes more cognitively complex.

> Even for low-skill occupations, job experience does not lead to convergence in performance among persons with different cognitive ability.

> For intellectually demanding jobs, there is no point at which more cognitive ability doesn't make a difference. Increases in IQ scores are statistically associated with increases in productivity at every level of cognitive ability.

You will find brilliant performers of every race in any occupation. That doesn't negate the relevance of these considerations to group means.

The magnitude of the relationship of cognitive ability to job performance varies. *Magnitude* in this case is usually expressed as the correlation coefficient between IQ and a measure of job performance. A correlation coefficient goes from –1 (a perfectly inverse relationship) to +1 (a perfectly direct relationship). The square of a correlation represents the percentage of the variance it "explains." Rules of thumb are that the correlations between IQ scores and job productivity for low-complexity jobs are seldom below .2; for medium-complexity jobs, they are seldom below .4; for high-complexity jobs, they are seldom below .5. Correlations of this size are too small to determine how well a given individual performs (even a correlation of .5 explains only 25 percent of the variance), but they are more than large enough to make cognitive ability an important element of an employee's productivity from the employer's point of view.

If you're an employer and want to know whether it's worth the trouble to give cognitive tests to job applicants, information about the correlation of IQ and productivity for a specific occupation makes it a straightforward matter to calculate the dollar value of hiring someone with an IQ of 100 versus someone with an IQ of 115. The difference might be too small to repay the bother of administering even a short written test; it may be large enough to warrant repeated interviews to assess an applicant's intellectual strengths.

I am not contending that a few points difference in IQ among employees is important. Rather, if one race in an occupation has mean cognitive ability that is conspicuously different from the mean cognitive ability of another race in the same job category in the same workplace, there are consequences for the productivity of an organization and also for the interactions of employees. Another consequence is the generalizations that people will draw from those differences.

In what follows, I document the existence of large race differences in cognitive ability in specific occupations. But first I will describe the ways in which the educational pipeline works to promote those differences.

## THE EDUCATIONAL PIPELINE

For jobs that require a college degree, race differences in cognitive ability in the workplace should be minimized by the process of obtaining that college degree. But it hasn't worked that way since at least the 1970s. Colleges have been complicit in transmitting the mean IQ differences by race in the general population not only through the college pipeline but through the graduate-education pipeline as well.

### Undergraduate Education

There is no reason that the means and distributions of cognitive ability in universities need to be different for Europeans, Africans, Latins, and Asians. If admissions committees made their decisions without knowing the applicants' races, all of those groups on a given campus would have roughly the same means and distributions on the SAT or the ACT. Not exactly the same, but in the same ballpark. That would be true of students of different races in the Ivies, flagship state universities, second-tier universities, and small colleges. There would be no basis for covert jokes about affirmative-action students, because it's not just test scores that would be similar across races. So would performance in the classroom.

The cost of implementing such a policy is that fewer

African and Latin students would be at the most prestigious colleges, but that cost would be counterbalanced by the greater presence of talented African and Latin students at other colleges. Young people of all races would be admitted to colleges where they were fully competitive with their fellow students. This would be apparent to everyone, with wonderful effects for authentic mutual respect among students. Yet admissions offices everywhere insist on having "enough" minority students, with the result that race differences in mean cognitive ability in the general population are replicated on campus.

Universities do their best to hide what's going on. They refuse to reveal mean SAT scores by race, proclaiming that "everyone we admit can do the work." What they don't acknowledge is that the admitted African and Latin students, as groups, will be concentrated in the bottom of their classes – and that the people making the admissions decisions know it in advance.

Occasionally, sunlight penetrates the darkness. The biggest leak occurred in late February 1993, when Richard Herrnstein, a professor at Harvard and my coauthor on *The Bell Curve*, arrived at his office one morning to find that someone had anonymously left a copy of the "Red Book" on his desk. At that time, the Red Book was produced annually by the Consortium on Financing Higher Education, which consisted of 16 out of the top 20 universities and 5 of the top 10 small colleges as ranked by *US News* for 1993. It was the university equivalent of leaking a Top Secret CIA document. The Red Book contained the mean SAT scores by race for each of the schools.

The median edge given to African applicants at those elite schools was about 180 points on the combined SAT, equivalent to approximately 1.3 standard deviations at the time – a larger gap than separated Africans and Europeans in the general population. Someone with an SAT score 1.3

standard deviations below the mean is at the 10th percentile of the distribution at those colleges. We published the school-by-school information in *The Bell Curve.*

Nothing seems to have changed since then. We don't have a current version of the Red Book to work with, but testimony in the recent case charging Harvard with discrimination against Asian applicants included evidence that the same profile of test scores, GPA, and extracurricular activities that gave an Asian applicant a 25 percent chance of admission gave an African applicant a 95 percent chance and a Latin a 77 percent chance.

This phenomenon wouldn't be important if it were limited to the elite schools, which admit a tiny fraction of all undergraduates. But universities draw from the talent pool in a hierarchy. African and Latin students with combined SATs in the 1500s are admitted everywhere they apply, but they tend to accept the most elite school on their list. Harvard, Princeton, and Yale have a lot of extraordinarily talented minority students, and they thin out the pool for the next schools in line. Even without a Red Book, it is easy to guess what then happens throughout the system. We can use a combination of two indicators, both of which are available in the *US News* rankings of universities: the percentages of African and Latin students in the undergraduate student body, and the SAT scores for the 25th, 50th, and 75th percentiles of admitted students.

Here it would be misleading to use the IQ metric because students who take the SAT and the ACT are self-selected for cognitive ability – they all want to attend a selective four-year institution. I am switching to $z$-scores, which represent where the racial means fall on the distribution of 17-year-olds and 18-year-olds who take the test. Recall from Chapter 3 that $z$-scores are expressed in standard deviations and that a standard deviation of 1 is equivalent to 15 points in the IQ metric.

| | Test Year | Mean Expressed in $z$-Scores | | | |
|---|---|---|---|---|---|
| | | European | African | Latin | Asian |
| SAT | 2020 | 0.25 | −0.59 | −0.39 | 0.79 |
| ACT | 2020 | 0.24 | −0.66 | −0.36 | 0.73 |
| *The national population* | | *0.20* | *−0.60* | *−0.40* | *0.53* |

The scores for both the SAT and the ACT match closely with the national estimates for Europeans, Africans, and Latins presented in Chapter 3, while Asians score well above their national estimate. That is, the SAT and ACT differences in means are about the same or greater among college applicants than they are in the population as a whole.

One implication of these results is that the raw numbers of African and Latin applicants with the minimum qualifications required for entry to an elite school are small, and that is indeed the case. For practical purposes, European and Asian applicants to elite schools need at least 1500 on their combined SATs, and well above that for the top tier – roughly the Ivies plus Stanford, Duke, MIT, Caltech, and Chicago. The College Board declined my request for the data that would give me the precise numbers, but the published breakdowns allow for reasonably accurate estimates of how many students of each race get 1500 or higher on the SAT.[1] The numbers of test takers with a combined verbal and math score of 1500+ were around 900 for Africans and around 3,300 for Latins. Meanwhile, the numbers for Europeans and Asians with scores in that range were about 27,500 and 20,000 respectively.

The result is that a large majority of Africans and Latins with combined SAT scores in the 1500s are swept up by the top tier. The rest of those top-scoring students and a large majority of those who score in the 1400s are in the next dozen schools in the *US News* or *Forbes* rankings. Ergo, many fine schools within the top 50 universities have virtually no African students with scores of 1400 or above, but still have large numbers of European and Asian students with scores not just in the 1400s but in the 1500s. Many good universities below the top 50 have no African students with scores as high as the 1300s but some European and Asian students with scores in the 1400s and 1500s.[2] Like the elite schools, they want to have a racially diverse student body. The result is a cascading propagation of a large difference in the mean cognitive ability of African, European, and Asian undergraduates all the way down the line from elite schools to ordinary ones. The same dynamics apply to Latin applicants but not as severely.

### Applications to Professional Schools

Table 5 below summarizes recent test scores for students who want to go into one of the professions by way of a medical degree, law degree, MBA, or PhD. For practical purposes, everyone who wants to get into one of these programs takes the Medical College Admission Test (MCAT), the Law School Admission Test (LSAT), or the Graduate Record Examinations (GRE). I show the $z$-score of the average applicant on the major test used for the professional field that the applicant wants to enter. *STEM* refers to science, technology, engineering, and mathematics.

The average difference between Europeans and Africans on these tests was larger than the IQ difference in the general population. The same was true of the Asian and African comparison. In contrast, Latins taking these tests had somewhat *smaller* differences with Europeans and Asians than Latins in the general population.

In terms of percentiles, Africans are in the bottom quartile of test scores for all the admissions tests except for

Table 5
Race Differences in Admissions Tests for Professional Training

| | Mean Expressed in $z$-Scores | | | |
| --- | --- | --- | --- | --- |
| | European | African | Latin | Asian |
| Medical School | 0.15 | −0.91 | −0.63 | 0.25 |
| Law School | 0.20 | −0.88 | −0.44 | 0.20 |
| MBA Programs | 0.14 | −0.65 | −0.31 | 0.09 |
| STEM PhD Programs | | | | |
|   Physical Sciences | 0.03 | −0.99 | −0.46 | 0.41 |
|   Life Sciences | 0.08 | −0.80 | −0.36 | 0.32 |
|   Engineering | 0.09 | −1.02 | −0.55 | 0.32 |
| Other PhD Programs | | | | |
|   Education | 0.20 | −0.59 | −0.35 | 0.10 |
|   Social & Behavioral Sciences | 0.15 | −0.72 | −0.38 | 0.06 |
|   Humanities | 0.11 | −0.82 | −0.56 | 0.01 |
| *The national population* | 0.20 | −0.60 | −0.40 | 0.53 |

those heading to business school or graduate school in education. The Latin scores are all in the second quartile.

### At the End of the Pipeline

One hopeful possibility remains: The admissions committees of graduate programs might cull the admitted pool so that the racial test-score gaps among those who actually matriculate are modest. Or perhaps the dropout rates mean that the people who eventually get PhDs, MDs, and JDs are much closer in ability than the applicants. The data for directly testing these possibilities are limited to medical school.

*Matriculation in Medical Schools.* The people who administer the MCAT are unique in reporting not only the test scores of the applicants but also the test scores of those who are accepted and matriculate. Here are the results for 2019:

|  | Mean $z$-Scores | | | |
|  | European | African | Latin | Asian |
| --- | --- | --- | --- | --- |
| Applicants | 0.15 | −0.91 | −0.63 | 0.25 |
| Matriculants | 0.09 | −0.89 | −0.82 | 0.37 |

Not much happened between application and admission to affect the differences. The European–African difference was reduced slightly while the European–Latin difference increased. The Asian differences from the other three races all increased.

*U.S. Medical Licensing Exam (USMLE).* This examination is required for admission into most residency programs. "Step 1" of the USMLE measures whether the test taker can "understand and can apply important concepts of the sciences basic to the practice of medicine." It consists of seven 60-minute blocks administered over an eight-hour period. In effect, it is an exit test from medical school. Below are the Step 1 $z$-scores for 10,541 applicants to residency programs during 2014–2015 at the Zucker School of Medicine at Hofstra/Northwell on Long Island, New York.

|  | Mean $z$-Scores | | | |
|  | European | African | Latin | Asian |
| --- | --- | --- | --- | --- |
| Applicants | 0.15 | −0.48 | −0.30 | 0.04 |

The race differences on the USMLE are noticeably smaller than those for matriculants to medical school, though they remained substantial. Asians no longer had the highest scores. The European–African and European–Latin differences were just 0.64 and 0.45 standard deviations respectively. These results indicate that medical school does in fact eliminate the weakest students. I return to this issue when I discuss the evidence from professional certification tests.

## OBSERVED DIFFERENCES IN COGNITIVE ABILITY WITHIN OCCUPATIONS

We now turn from inferential data to the observed cognitive ability of people who are employed in various occupations. The question itself is simple: What's the mean IQ of Europeans employed as electrical engineers? High school teachers? Plumbers? What are the comparable mean IQs for African, Latin, and Asian electrical engineers, high school teachers, and plumbers?

Finding databases to answer the question is hard, however, because it requires analyzable sample sizes for individual occupations, which implies a study with large sample sizes and also a good measure of cognitive ability. The three such datasets that I found are the 1972 National Longitudinal Study sponsored by the Department of Education and the 1979 and 1997 cohorts of the National Longitudinal Survey of Youth sponsored by the Department of Labor. The three cohorts combined give us 20,203 Europeans, Africans, and Latins whose occupations in their 30s and 40s are known, as are their scores on a $g$-loaded mental test that they took in their teens or early 20s. Unfortunately, the number of Asians in these studies was too small to provide reliable estimates of IQ for specific occupations.

The results you are about to see are based on persons who were born from the early 1950s through the early 1980s – people who as of 2021 are ages 37 to late 60s.

As you will recall from Chapter 3, the narrowing of the European–African gap occurred in tests administered from the late 1970s through the mid- to late-1980s, which in most cases involved people born before the early 1970s. Thus the members of the samples tested in 1972 and 1980 were born when both the European–African and the European–Latin differences were higher than they are now. The European differences in the 1972 and 1980 surveys were 1.29 and 1.24 SDs respectively, while the Latin–European differences were 0.99 and 0.93 SDs respectively. The sample tested in 1997 showed a smaller European–African difference of 0.98 SDs and a smaller European–Latin difference of 0.67. You should keep this in mind when you look at the numbers in Table 6. They accurately reflect the profile of the labor force for the last few decades, but the IQ differences among the younger members of the labor force are typically a few points smaller than the differences among the older members.

### *IQ Differences in Ordinary Jobs*

Comparatively few people are physicists, physicians, attorneys, or work in other high-prestige occupations, which means that even a sample of 20,203 includes too few in such occupations to provide analyzable samples by race for them. But the three studies do have enough people in more normal occupations to do so, and the sample weights used by the studies enable us to reach estimates that are representative of the national population, so I can return to using the IQ metric.

Table 6 below shows mean IQs and the sizes of the race differences for nine familiar occupations ranging from cognitively demanding (accountant) to a low-skill job (janitor or building cleaner). They are a selection from a larger set of occupations for which data are presented in the online documentation. I have ordered the occupations by the European mean IQ from highest to lowest.

Table 6
Race Differences in IQ Within Occupations

| | Mean IQ | | | Race Differences in SDs | |
| Occupation | European | African | Latin | European–African | European–Latin |
|---|---|---|---|---|---|
| Accountants | 111 | 100 | 104 | 0.96 | 0.60 |
| K–12 teachers | 110 | 95 | 101 | 1.35 | 0.76 |
| Registered nurses | 109 | 94 | 105 | 1.49 | 0.42 |
| Social workers | 105 | 95 | 93 | 0.93 | 1.09 |
| Retail sales workers | 102 | 89 | 93 | 1.17 | 0.80 |
| Childcare workers | 102 | 83 | 85 | 1.55 | 1.34 |
| Secretaries & AAs | 102 | 90 | 93 | 0.96 | 0.72 |
| Vehicle mechanics | 94 | 83 | 87 | 0.85 | 0.57 |
| Janitors & bldg. cleaners | 92 | 79 | 82 | 1.10 | 0.78 |
| Median | 102 | 90 | 93 | 1.10 | 0.76 |
| Mean | 103 | 90 | 94 | 1.15 | 0.79 |

With just one exception (vehicle mechanics), all of the European–African differences are greater than the 0.85 SD national estimate from Chapter 3. The mean difference is 1.15 SDs. The differences for registered nurses, K–12 teachers, and childcare workers are especially large. The European–Latin differences are closer to the estimated national difference of 0.62 SDs, with an average over all nine occupations of 0.79 SDs.

76

Table 7 below expands the power of the analysis by grouping occupations that are filled by people with similar IQs. For example, the combined samples do not have enough African or Latin physicians to provide reliable estimates, but combining them with other occupations that draw from people with mean IQs above 115 – college teachers and lawyers, for example – increases the samples to usable sizes.

The IQ groupings in Table 7 are based on the European mean. Categories below 100 are all blue-collar jobs, ranging from unskilled to highly skilled labor. The 100–104 category includes occupations for which the European mean was at least 100 and less than 105. Examples are preschool teachers, police, and electricians. Examples of occupations in the 105–109 category are registered nurses, secretaries, and social workers. Examples of occupations in the 110–114 category are accountants, clergy, computer programmers, and engineers. Examples of occupations in the 115+ category are physicians, dentists, lawyers, and college teachers.

The mean IQs of Africans and Latins increase with each higher category, just as the European means do, but the size

### Table 7
#### Race Differences in Occupations Grouped by the European Mean

| IQ Group | Mean | | | Difference in Standard Deviations | |
| --- | --- | --- | --- | --- | --- |
| | European | African | Latin | European–African | European–Latin |
| 90–94 | 93 | 82 | 85 | 0.98 | 0.67 |
| 95–100 | 97 | 85 | 88 | 1.02 | 0.70 |
| 100–105 | 103 | 88 | 93 | 1.15 | 0.77 |
| 105–109 | 107 | 95 | 97 | 1.02 | 0.83 |
| 110–114 | 113 | 99 | 104 | 1.21 | 0.73 |
| 115+ | 118 | 105 | 112 | 1.11 | 0.53 |

of the difference generally keeps pace. In the case of the European–African difference, the size of the difference tends to increase along with IQ, from 1.01 SDs for occupations with European mean IQs under 100 to 1.20 SDs for European mean IQs of 110 or higher.

Why are employers ending up with workforces in which the differences in cognitive ability are so large? The answers probably vary for different occupations, illustrated by some of the occupations in Table 6.

*Janitors and building cleaners.* For unskilled occupations, a substantial part of the difference is a statistically predictable phenomenon. It occurs when almost all of the population is "smart enough" to do a particular job, the races have different IQ means, and employers also value noncognitive qualifications such as reliability. This explains much of the 13-point difference between European and African janitors. As the cognitive demands of occupations increase, the importance of that statistical phenomenon drops. For occupations of greater complexity that have a lower-bound IQ requirement near 100, only a small proportion of the differences in Table 6 and Table 7 can be consistent with a fair hiring process that ignores race.

*Childcare workers.* One plausible explanation of the large European–African difference of 1.55 SDs is that noncognitive traits such as warmth, reliability, and "being good with children" become extremely important in choosing a childcare worker and outweigh considerations of cognitive ability. Another plausible explanation is that the requirements for being hired as a childcare worker vary by the socioeconomic status of the neighborhood. In neighborhoods with affluent and highly educated parents, nannies and preschool programs are supposed to provide cognitive stimulation to the children – a priority that can reach comical heights in high-status neighborhoods where getting one's children into the right preschool is seen as the essential first step for getting them into Princeton. The result may be that the cognitive requirements and the pay for childcare workers in affluent neighborhoods are far higher than they are for childcare workers in poor neighborhoods.

*Registered nurses and K–12 teachers.* The European–African differences are 1.49 SDs for registered nurses and 1.35 SDs for K–12 teachers. Part of the explanation is probably as simple as demand outstripping supply. Shortages of nurses and teachers mean that hospitals and schools don't have the option of being choosy. But another plausible explanation involves a potentially good thing – a certification requirement – in combination with the way that anti-discrimination employment laws are administered.

To become registered nurses, graduates of nursing schools must pass an examination, usually the NCLEX-RN. In almost all states, K–12 teachers are also required to take examinations (which vary by state) to be hired as teachers.

The granting of certification is typically based on pass/ fail with no gradations. You either get your certification or you don't. This is appropriate for establishing a minimum level of competence, but it means that the people who pass the test represent a wide range of performance, from the barely qualified to the superbly qualified. If they could, most hospitals and most school systems would presumably want to choose the most qualified. But to do so would leave them vulnerable to lawsuits and investigation by the Equal Employment Opportunity Commission if the people they hired turned out to be disproportionately European.

This is not the place to describe the murky jurisprudence surrounding the use of tests in employment decisions (the online documentation has a summary). An employer cannot be certain that hiring people with the highest scores on a certification test will cause trouble, but it is a strong possibility if the employer ends up hiring too many Europeans and Asians among the pool of people who passed the exam. In effect, the employer is arguing that a yes/no standard of "qualified" is inadequate for employment decisions – a heavy legal burden.

This situation applies to all certification tests – the Certified Public Accountant exam, bar exams, board certifications for physicians, qualification exams for promotion in police and fire departments, along with certification tests for registered nurses and K–12 teachers. A workforce may consist entirely of people who have passed the exam and still have large race differences in the scores of the people who passed. Since the examinations themselves are inevitably correlated with $g$ to some extent, the result is differences in mean IQ of the sizes seen in Tables 6 and 7.

### *Differences in the Hiring Pools for Extremely High-IQ Jobs*

I turn now to an issue that involves only a tiny proportion of the workforce but has high visibility: the rarity of Africans and Latins in the most prestigious jobs in the private sector. That rarity is often used as undeniable evidence of systemic racism in the job market.

Many of those high-prestige jobs are filled by people not merely in the top few percentiles of cognitive ability, but well into the top percentile. Recall the discussion of the "width" of the top percentile of a bell curve in Chapter 3 – LeBron James is in the same percentile as starting players on ordinary college teams. The same phenomenon applies to an oncologist in an ordinary practice and the chief of oncology at a major research hospital. The former may be an excellent oncologist, but the latter has undergone a severe winnowing process that among other things has selected specifically for evidence of intellectual brilliance. Other examples of positions that select for extremely high cognitive ability are:

> A full professorship at an elite university

> A senior position in the financial industry

> A senior position in the IT industry

> Law partner in a major firm in a major city

> CEO of a major corporation

This is not to say that intellectually brilliant people typically have important jobs in a society – on the contrary, few do – but that a characteristic of people who rise to the top in every cognitively demanding profession in elite academia and elite organizations in the private sector is exceptionally high cognitive ability. I will operationalize *exceptionally high* as a minimum IQ of 135. High-prestige jobs in government and the nonprofit sector are also sometimes filled by exceptionally able people, but the rigor of the screening process varies a lot by job and organization.

Why are there so few minorities in these high-prestige jobs? It's a numbers game in which the odds against a Latin achieving one of those positions are high and the odds against an African are prohibitive, even if we assume that there is no racism whatsoever among the employers for high-prestige jobs.

To illustrate, I'll use the cohort of young Americans ages 25–29, the age at which the potential candidates for such jobs are coming out of law schools, medical schools, business schools, and graduate STEM departments. In 2019, there were 23.2 million Americans in that age group. About 228,000 people in that age group can be expected to have IQs of 135 or higher.

The racial distribution of Americans ages 25–29 in 2019 was more multiracial than among the older population. Only 54 percent were European while 20 percent were

Latin, 15 percent were African, and 6 percent were Asian. But that reduced dominance of Europeans in the total population doesn't make a lot of difference in the 135+ pool. Employers seeking these exceptionally intelligent young adults were choosing from a pool that contained only about 2,800 Africans and 9,500 Latins compared to 50,700 Asians and 160,100 Europeans. (Uncertainty about these numbers arises because the standard deviation for each race must be estimated.)

As in the case of admissions at elite universities, we can assume that the most prestigious employers snagged disproportionate numbers of the most talented new graduates. Given the number of employers and the sizes of the different racial pools, the inevitable result was that a large majority of U.S. employers that seek out new hires with 135+ IQs had no entry-level Africans or Latins among those hires. Zero, no matter how eagerly the employers solicited minority candidates. There weren't enough to meet the demand.

Why aren't there more Africans and Latins in senior positions in the corporations and institutions that did hire such talented people? Again, it's a numbers game. Let's say that an elite IT company in Silicon Valley snags 100 new hires from the 135+ pool in the racial proportions of the pool as a whole. That means 70 are European, 22 are Asian, 4 are Latin, 1 is African, and 3 are a mixture of races or "other." What percent of new hires of any race in any company rise to senior positions? It depends on the organization, and the definition of senior, but in any case the four Latins are competing against 96 others and the one African is competing against 99 others to become one of the chosen few. Those are daunting odds.

Unless you are familiar with race differences in cognitive ability, you might reasonably be convinced that the absence of African and Latin faces in the highest ranks of the American private sector means that you live in a systemically racist country. If instead you are familiar with those differences and you still want to expose racism wherever it does exist, you will start your inquiries aware that it is *inevitable* that a large majority of employers of people with extremely high cognitive ability will have no Africans or Latins in those coveted jobs. Among those that do have some Africans or Latins, only a small minority will have even one in the upper echelons of the organization. These results will occur in the absence of any racism whatsoever.

## The Relationship of Differences in Cognitive Ability to Job Performance

Many readers probably have reached this point in the discussion with a variant on the question that they had after the discussion of test scores in Chapter 3. Then, the question was whether IQ scores fairly represent the cognitive ability of minorities. Now, the question is whether differences in cognitive ability translate into significant differences in job performance and productivity. What does it mean for the quality of customer service when one group of retail salespersons has a mean IQ 13 points lower than another group? What does it mean for children's education if one group of K–12 teachers has a mean IQ that is 15 points lower than another group?

### Results from Job Performance Meta-Analyses

We cannot answer such questions directly through meta-analyses because the studies of race differences in job performance seldom have measures of both job performance and cognitive ability. Rather, we know that IQ and job performance are correlated in analyses without regard to race. We know that people of different races in the same occupations have substantially different cognitive ability. Given those two knowns, it is reasonable to expect that the literature on race and job performance will consistently show that race differences exist, and in fact this has been the case.

The two most comprehensive meta-analyses are by Philip L. Roth, Allen Huffcutt, and Philip Bobko, "Ethnic Group Differences in Measures of Job Performance: A New Meta-Analysis," published in the *Journal of Applied Psychology* (2003); and by Patrick F. McKay and Michael A. McDaniel, "A Reexamination of Black-White Mean Differences in Work Performance: More Data, More Moderators," published in the *Journal of Applied Psychology* (2006). Their findings build on early synthetic analyses from the 1980s and 1990s and are consistent with each other. These generalizations are well established:

> ▸ European–African differences in job performance are found for jobs at all levels of cognitive complexity, with a mild tendency for the size of the difference to increase with complexity.

> ▸ Objective measures of job performance and subjective ratings of job performance show roughly similar differences.

> ▸ On average, measures of performance related to personality (e.g., prosocial behaviors on the job) showed small race differences; the larger the cognitive component of the measure (e.g., job knowledge), the greater the size of race differences.

The size of the European–African differences in job performance varies depending on the occupation and the measure. The Roth and the McKay studies both put the average at about a third of a standard deviation. These differences are consistent with expectations if the correlation between IQ and job performance measures is in the range discussed earlier (generally .2 to .5).

An intriguing bright spot is the military's record. A large 1989 study of performance ratings among Army enlisted personnel found that Europeans had a modest advantage over Africans on measures of task proficiency and job effort, but there was little difference on measures of discipline and an African advantage on measures of military bearing. There was no meaningful difference on any of the measures for Europeans and Latins. The McKay meta-analysis, which was limited to the European–African comparison, included results from five studies of military personnel. The Europeans still had an advantage on work quality measures, but the combined measures of job performance led to an overall European–African difference of –0.09; in other words, a small African advantage.

Results for the military stand apart from all civilian work settings and occupations. One relevant factor for explaining the military's success is presumably that each branch has its own minimum score on the Armed Forces Qualification Test required of all recruits. The Army requires a score at the 31st percentile or higher, equivalent to an IQ of 92.6 or more, which is roughly the top half of the African and Latin distributions. Presumably another factor is that military personnel cannot train for the military occupational specialty of their choice unless they have high enough scores on the relevant subtests in the Armed Services Vocational Aptitude Battery. Technically, there's no reason that civilian employers that used comparable procedures couldn't achieve similar results. However, doing so would mean basing employment decisions not only on an IQ cutoff but also on aptitude tests, both of which run the risk of violating the antidiscrimination laws that apply to civilians.

*Results for Specific Occupations*

Averages from meta-analyses don't tell you anything about specific occupations. Those numbers are hard to come by. I managed to assemble some bits and pieces. The details are in the note, but I can summarize the results quickly.[3]

Among accountants, race differences in the pass rate for the Certified Public Accountant exam are commensurate with the race differences in cognitive ability.

In the legal profession, the race differences in pass rates for the bar exam are commensurate with race differences in cognitive ability. So are differences in the percentage of attorneys who have been the subject of repeated complaints in California.

In the medical profession, race differences in board certification for a medical specialty are commensurate with race differences in cognitive ability. So are differences in investigations of complaints filed against physicians, and in disciplinary action by the state medical board of California.

For K–12 teachers, race differences among those rated "minimally effective" or "ineffective" in Michigan were commensurate with race differences in cognitive ability.

I wish that I could give you more systematic, nationwide evidence bearing on professional competence. The evidence from the bits and pieces is given credibility by its consistency with the findings of the meta-analyses, but if nonetheless the bits and pieces are misleading it should be easy to prove. The archives of city and state agencies, legal and medical professional organizations, and the federal government contain voluminous data on bar examinations and medical board certifications, on legal and medical malpractice, on police performance ratings, on teachers' ratings, and on performance measures for other occupations

**Figure 1**
**America's Racial**
**Concentrations in 2019**

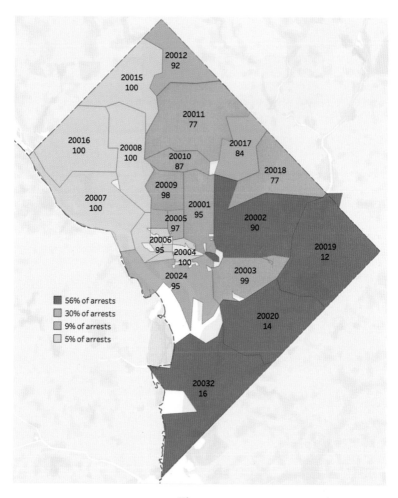

Figure 2
Arrests for Violent Offenses in the District of Columbia
and Socioeconomic Status by Zip Code

# Figure 3

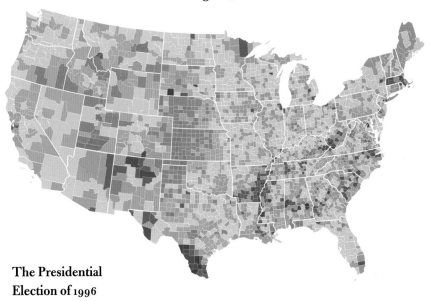

The Presidential
Election of 1996

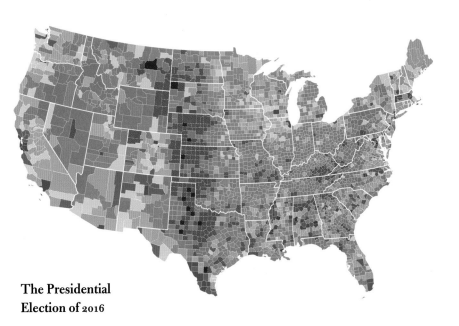

The Presidential
Election of 2016

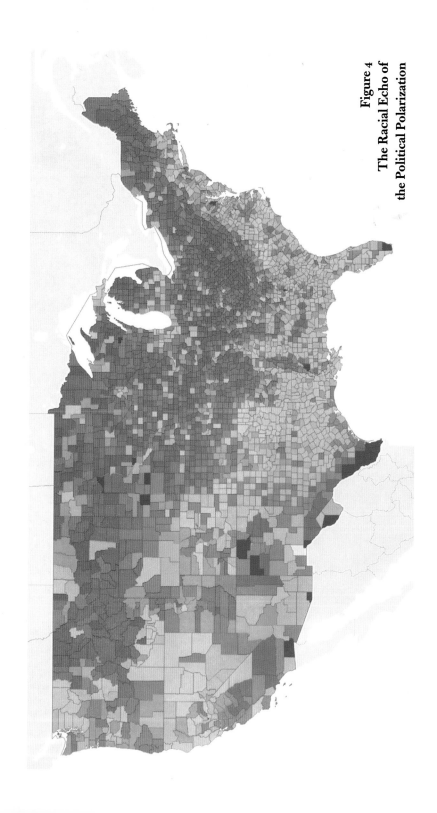

Figure 4
The Racial Echo of
the Political Polarization

requiring licensing or monitoring. There's no shortage of evidence that could confirm or refute my presentation. That evidence just hasn't been made available for public examination. As for the occupations that don't require licensing or monitoring, every major corporation in the country has detailed records on job performance. They know exactly how those records differ by race. If any of them has a success story similar to the military's, I hope they will tell it and explain how it was done.

## SYSTEMIC RACIAL PREFERENCES IN THE JOB MARKET

The usual way in which the media and politicians talk about race discrimination in the job market is to compare the percentage of Africans or Latins in a given occupation with the percentage of Europeans. This makes the situation look bad. The 2014–2018 American Community Survey found that Africans, at 13 percent of the population, accounted for only 3.6 percent of CEOs, 3.7 percent of physical scientists, 4.4 percent of civil engineers, 5.1 percent of physicians, and 5.2 percent of lawyers. Latin percentages in those prestigious occupations ranged from 5.3 to 7.6 percent, but Latins are almost 18 percent of the population, so their underrepresentation was nearly the same.

The picture flips when race differences in cognitive ability and job performance are taken into account. Africans and Latins get through the educational pipeline with preferential treatment in admissions to colleges and to professional programs. Their mean IQs in occupations across the range from unskilled to those requiring advanced degrees are substantially lower than the mean IQs for Europeans in the same occupations. Race differences in measures of on-the-job performance are commensurate with the differences in cognitive ability.

I think it is fair to conclude that the American job market is indeed racially biased. A detached observer might even call it systemic racism. The American job market systemically discriminates in favor of racial minorities other than Asians.

CHAPTER SIX

# First-Order Effects
# of Race Differences in Crime

RACE DIFFERENCES in crime rates have different effects in different places. In big cities, race differences in crime rates have broad effects on the social structure and functioning of the city and on policing in particular. In towns and small cities, those effects are much less pronounced and sometimes nonexistent.

## EFFECTS IN BIG-CITY AMERICA

Race differences in crime have more effects in big cities than in towns and small cities because all of them have a part of town where each of the two races with higher crime rates is residentially concentrated. Among the fifty-two places I defined in Chapter 2 as big-city America, with 500,000 people or more in a contiguous urban area, even the smallest African population (15,600 in Albuquerque) and the smallest Latin population (17,100 in Pittsburgh) are large enough to form distinctly African or Latin neighborhoods, though in comparatively small parts of town. In 2019 the median number of Africans in the fifty-two big cities was 226,500 and the median number of Latins was

89

173,900 – enough to create African and Latin parts of town so large that they have their own shopping and entertainment districts. The poorest neighborhoods within them, which also tend to be the ones with the highest crime rates, are called the "inner city."

The nation's capital provides a classic example of the result. Figure 2 in the insert shows the zip codes of the District of Columbia and their socioeconomic status (SES). The top number is the zip code. The bottom number is the zip code's percentile on an index that combines the zip code's median family income and the percentage of adults in that zip code with at least a college degree. Percentiles have been rounded to the nearest whole number. Thus the five zip codes with index scores of 100 are in the top half of the 99th percentile relative to the rest of the population of the United States.

Of all the arrests for violent crimes from 2013 to 2019, 56 percent occurred in the four zip codes colored red. Another 30 percent of them occurred in the six codes colored orange. That leaves just 14 percent to be divided among all the zip codes colored blue. A large swathe of Washington with the highest socioeconomic status experienced just 5 percent of the arrests.

The insulation of Washington's elites from violent crime is even greater than the map indicates. Three of the orange zip codes are partially gentrified. Zip code 20003 includes Capitol Hill. The zip code as a whole is in the 99th percentile of SES despite having a large low-income population in its eastern half. A microanalysis of the geocodes reveals that the bulk of the arrests occurred in the eastern half of zip code 20003. The same is true of zip codes 20001 and 20009 – the zip codes manage to have such high SES rankings despite being divided into affluent and low-income neighborhoods. Most of the arrests that cause the zip codes to be colored orange occurred in the ungentrified parts. I use Washington as the example (perhaps partly because I lived in zip codes 20003 and 20009 for a total of nine years), but the pattern applies to New York City, Los Angeles, and Chicago as well. That pattern – a high concentration of crime in the poorest part of town – creates a variety of effects.

### *Effects on Economic Activity*

In big-city America, disproportionate minority crime rates cause Europeans and Asians to avoid going into minority neighborhoods. Crime rates and socioeconomic status both vary widely across zip codes in minority neighborhoods in big-city America. These areas contain middle-class zip codes and impoverished ones; zip codes with low crime rates and others with high crime rates. But that makes no difference to the perception held by most Europeans and Asians. Unfamiliar with these variations, they typically see the entire minority part of town as potentially dangerous. It's not a matter of simple racism. The same Europeans and Asians who avoid going to the minority part of town may have minority colleagues at work with whom they get along fine. They may have minority neighbors with whom they are friends. But they won't go to the minority part of town to shop, stay at a hotel, buy a car, or send their children to school. They don't drive into it unless it is the shortest route to someplace they need to go.

They also won't buy a home in the minority part of town unless they are pioneers initiating gentrification or are taking advantage of gentrification that is already well underway, but it would be a mistake to think they are deterred only because of crime. Widespread and voluntary residential segregation by race seems to be a fact of life around the world, no matter what the races are or what the country's economic and political system is. In discussing the effects of crime, I am referring specifically to economic effects.

*In big-city America, disproportionate minority crime rates deter developers from building office space in minority neighborhoods unless gentrification is already well underway.* Real estate is typically cheaper in African or Latin parts of town than elsewhere, a factor that would ordinarily attract developers to build office space for law firms, doctors' offices, and other businesses that would like to escape the high rentals in the European midtown. But unless it is clear that the neighborhood is near a gentrification tipping point, those lucrative rentals won't happen, and so the office buildings don't get built.

*In big-city America, disproportionate minority crime rates raise the costs of doing business for retailers of all kinds.* It is often alleged that large commercial chains avoid putting stores in minority neighborhoods. The empirical part of the allegation is sometimes true, but the inference that racism is to blame does not follow. Shoplifting is far more common in many big-city minority neighborhoods than elsewhere. It often doesn't make economic sense for big chain stores, which have business models based on low profit margins, to locate in such neighborhoods. Either they won't make a profit or they will have to charge higher prices, leaving themselves open to accusations of racist price gouging. If they take measures to apprehend shoplifters, they risk charges of racism and financial shakedowns through the threat of lawsuits. Actions taken to prevent shoplifting can also put employees at risk of violent confrontations. It's a no-win situation. Opening a store in a big-city minority neighborhood is often not economically rational. Racism need not have anything to do with the decision.

Meanwhile, the small locally owned retailers in a big-city minority neighborhood also have a hard time making a profit because of shoplifting, the threat of robbery, high insurance costs, and banks' reluctance to make high-risk loans. The locally owned stores tend to be poorly stocked, with few amenities, and overpriced relative to stores selling the same goods elsewhere.

*Effects on Policy Interventions*

The problems of America's inner cities have preoccupied policy analysts for fifty years. Many reforms have been proposed and many attempts at implementing them have received generous government funding. The dismal record of those efforts has been widely recognized by policy scholars across the political spectrum. Their failures have been intimately linked with the high crime rates in the neighborhoods where the efforts have been undertaken.

*High minority crime rates make many policy solutions inherently unrealistic.* Among the reasons that inner-city reform programs have so consistently failed is that the desired objective is directly impeded by the existence of high crime. Raj Chetty of Harvard and his colleagues have conducted extremely detailed geographic analyses of upward socioeconomic mobility down to the level of city blocks. They have been able to identify certain characteristics of neighborhoods that matter. One is a low level of racial bias among local Europeans, and another is a high level of social interaction across racial groups. But neighborhoods with high minority crime rates are intrinsically places where "racial bias among local Europeans" will be high and where social interaction across racial groups will be low. No government program can change that.

Other social interventions for helping inner-city children and adolescents come up against similar inherent problems. Preschool for toddlers, mentoring for young men without fathers, educational enrichment, counseling services – all of these have a chance of making a contribution if they are implemented in neighborhoods where they are reinforced by large numbers of functional two-parent families. But African and Latin parents in such families have exactly the same priority as those in functional two-parent European and Asian families: Do everything possible to find a safe place to raise their children. The result is that most of them have left high-crime areas for other neighborhoods and that the sponsors of the interventions do *not* have large numbers of functional two-parent families to reinforce their efforts. The places where the need for social interventions is greatest are the places where they have the least chance of working. High crime is a big part of the reason.

*Attempts to stimulate economic growth in places with high crime rates work only in places that are gentrifying or can be gentrified.* Over the decades since the 1960s, federal and municipal governments have periodically introduced programs that offer economic incentives for businesses to invest in the inner city. The most recent example consists of the Opportunity Zones enacted as part of the Tax Cuts and Jobs Act of 2017. The act offers capital-gains tax breaks for investments in about 8,700 designated Opportunity Zones, supposedly in disadvantaged areas (it is reported that some of them aren't), with the intention of spurring economic growth and job creation. The academic analyses of the results so far suggest that this initiative is producing the same unintended outcomes that have characterized previous efforts.

Some of these results are endemic to government programs intended to help the disadvantaged – the process is captured by politicians, lawyers, consultants, and lobbyists who successfully game the rules. But attempts to stimulate economic growth in the inner city are vulnerable to a specific, built-in opportunity for exploitation: The land occupied by the inner city really is potentially worth a lot of money if – but only if – the minority residents are replaced through gentrification. Thus big cities throughout the

94

country have seen neighborhoods that were notorious centers of crime, drugs, and desperate poverty become fashionable, high-priced parts of town through gentrification. Property values soared. So did the availability of jobs. But this was of scant benefit to those who had lived there, few of whom had been owners of that newly valuable property and few of whom filled the new jobs.

Each new attempt to revitalize inner cities *for the people who already live there* has run up against this built-in obstacle. In the case of the Opportunity Zones, the capital-gains tax benefits have led to increased property values for vacant lots and property designated for redevelopment – but because of the monetary value of the tax benefit and the longer-term prospect of gentrification. The value of the shop next to the vacant lot has not increased, nor will the shop be hiring any more employees, because there has been no change in the economic attractiveness of that part of the city. A major reason is crime.

### *Effects on Policing*

The American criminal justice system needs reform on many fronts. Inconsistencies in sentencing, including racial injustices, are a problem. Uneven enforcement of drug laws is a problem. Overuse of imprisonment is a problem. The militarization of the police is a problem. Wrong and sometimes criminal behavior by police is a problem. Nothing that follows is intended to minimize those problems or to deny that racism still exists within the criminal justice system. Rather, I want to introduce some realism about what we can expect from normal, well-meaning human beings, trying to behave professionally and appropriately, in an environment of large race differences in violent criminality.

The job of a police patrol officer – a cop – in an urban setting is unique. Many occupations involve close personal interactions with a wide variety of people. Many occupations have broadly defined goals and flexible rules, giving the worker wide discretion. A small number of occupations require decisions on matters of the utmost importance, including life and death. A still smaller number of occupations require that decisions sometimes be made within seconds. Only a handful of occupations are intrinsically dangerous.

The job of an urban police patrol officer is unique in combining all of those attributes. Any or all can be brought into play on any given shift. This is especially true of physical danger. Being a logger or a firefighter carries intrinsic physical risks, but only two ways of making a lawful living are intrinsically dangerous because other human beings may deliberately assault or kill you – being a member of a combat unit in the military or being a police officer.

The way the police officer's job looks to the outside world and the way it looks to the police are radically different. I spent all of Chapter 4 discussing a handful of the most serious crimes, but enforcement of the laws against the index crimes takes up only a tiny fraction of a patrol officer's time. Most of a cop's time and energy are spent on maintaining order. Disorder – the thing the police are supposed to fix – can be an obnoxious drunk, a homeless man berating passersby, teenagers blocking a sidewalk, a bar fight, a man pushing a woman around, someone dealing crystal meth, or a robber holding up a convenience store. Depending on the situation, the professionally correct police response spans the range from "Why don't you tell me your side of the story" to drawing a loaded weapon and firing it at a citizen.

That description doesn't begin to convey the range, complexity, and ambiguity of the situations that big-city police face all the time. Describing them adequately has been the topic of thick books. My point is that the environment in which cops work necessarily has an impact on the choices they make. As an empirical matter, a cop who politely suggests "go home and sober up" to a middle-class 45-year-old man on a suburban street who has had too much to drink has reason to be confident that whether the response is meek or belligerent, it will pose no serious physical danger. A 20-year-old male of any race in a high-crime neighborhood who has gotten equally drunk with some other 20-year-olds will probably acquiesce nonviolently, but there is a nontrivial chance that he or one of his friends will respond with a weapon. There is a nontrivial chance that the young males are not in an alcoholic stupor but strung out on ecstasy. Police in such situations are less confident that a polite request to go home will have the desired effect. The course they choose will reflect their need to protect against the possibility of a violent response.

Now think in terms of frequency distributions of the amount of force that police use. For every situation that a cop faces, let us say there is an optimal choice, as defined in the police training manuals or perhaps by an omniscient observer. As the environment in which police are working becomes more dangerous, that optimal choice moves along the distribution toward the use-more-force-and-defensive-precautions tail of the bell curve.

One result is that well-trained police exercising good judgment will, on average, take more steps to establish their authority, call for more backup, and respond with more force to provocations in high-crime parts of town than in low-crime areas, regardless of the race of the citizens they are dealing with.

Another result is that errors in judgment will be skewed toward the greater-force end of the distribution. If the error in the direction of greater force is perceived as reducing the downside risk, and the downside risk is one's own death, then police officers, being human, will err on the side of protecting themselves. Added to that human reaction is the mental stress associated with combat – stress unlike anything that most of us (including me) have ever experienced. The physiological effects of the adrenaline surge are powerful, and they are in addition to the psychological effects of fear and anger. All of these factors mean that police use of force, including excessive use of force, will always and inevitably be higher in high-crime areas than in low-crime areas, and high-crime areas in the United States are overwhelmingly urban and African or Latin.

These observations do not excuse the examples caught on video of police willfully harassing or physically mistreating African or Latin citizens. Police who do such things should be kicked off the force and shunned by other police departments. The problem is that those videos go viral, watched by millions. Those same millions do not see video from police body cameras showing the thousands of daily instances when police continue to be polite in the face of obscenities screamed at them, expose themselves to risk rather than overreact to a threat, or make extraordinary efforts to help someone who is injured or in danger.

What about the most outrageous and the most viral of all the videos, the ones that show police killing defenseless suspects? Those police are guilty of criminal acts that deserve the severest punishment. But to conflate them with errors in decisions that had to be made in seconds in the face of lethal threats is a libel on police. They deserve better of the people they serve.

## Effects in Small-City America

I have argued elsewhere that the differences between big-city America and everywhere else are the real cultural fault line that has polarized the nation. Life in big-city America is different on almost every dimension from life in rural, small-town, and small-city America. That is as true of the effects of race differences in crime rates as it is of everything else.

I will operationally define small-city America as stand-alone places of fewer than 150,000 people. "Stand-alone" means that they are not part of one of the 52 big-city contiguous urban areas. In all, 170 million people, more than half of the American population, live in small-city America. I use the label *small-city America* for convenience, but most of those people live in places that are more like towns than cities. Half of them live in rural areas or towns of less than 25,000, and another 20 percent of them live in cities of 25,000–50,000.

Race differences in crime rates in small-city America are less important than in big-city America. This is true partly because the violent crime rates are usually much lower. In 2017, the mean rate of violent offenses per hundred thousand in stand-alone cities of less than 150,000 population was 333 per 100,000 – less than half the mean rate of 679 in cities larger than that. The smaller the crime problem, the less ominous are race differences in crime rates.

It's not just that the crime rate is lower in towns and small cities. Race relations are likely to be different as well. It is possible for a city of under 150,000 to have a large minority neighborhood if the overall percentage of the minority is high, but that is uncommon. Far more often, the African or Latin neighborhood is small and more socially permeable than a minority neighborhood with tens of thousands of people covering many city blocks. In a town or small city, Europeans, Africans, and Latins are more likely to shop in the same stores and go to the same doctors' offices than in the megalopolises. They may not be more likely to worship together – apparently churches still constitute the most racially segregated institution in America – but they are more likely to volunteer for the same community activities and to be members of the same local civic institutions.

Perhaps most importantly, the children in small-city America are likely to grow up knowing people who don't look like them. If the minority community is small, none of the schools can be segregated in any meaningful sense. Parents of different races will attend the same PTA meetings and sit in the same bleachers for Little League games. About 100 million people who inhabit small-city America live in a place that has only one high school. All the high school students, of all races and socioeconomic classes, can be found in the same hallways, classrooms, lunchrooms, and on the same athletic teams.

A basic feature of human psychology makes all this relevant to the way that race differences in crime rates are perceived. It is easy to stereotype a race or any other kind of identifiable group if you do not actually know members of that group. Intimate friendships aren't required. Just acquaintance and regular interaction go a long way toward defusing the stereotype. When it comes to crime rates, the typical experience of Europeans in small-city America is to have encountered and gotten to know at least several members of a given minority over the years. Statistically, odds are that none of them is any scarier than the European is. It's one thing to be aware in the abstract that only a small proportion of the members of any race are violent or criminal. It's a much different thing to know from experience that only a small proportion – usually zero – of the members of a given minority that you know personally are violent or criminal.

These general characteristics of towns and small cities play out somewhat differently in different parts of small-city America.

## CHAPTER SIX

### *European Small-City America*

Almost 67 million Americans live in rural areas, towns, or cities of under 150,000 where at least 85 percent of the local population is European. In these places, the violent crime rate (using 2017 data) is 58 per 100,000, one-sixth of the national average. Another 33 million Americans live in places where 75–84 percent of the population is European. Their average violent crime rate is 126 per 100,000, a third of the national average.

These crime rates are too low to make race an issue in how these communities function on any dimension, no matter what the ratio of African/European or Latin/European crime rates might be. That's a total of 100 million Americans for whom race differences in crime rates are irrelevant to their daily lives.

### *African Small-City America*

To qualify as a part of African small-city America requires that Africans be at least 25 percent of the population and also be the largest minority in the town or city. Sixteen million Americans live in places meeting that definition. Overall, 42 percent of the population of African small-city America is African. The violent crime rate in those places averages 401 per 100,000.

While that rate is just slightly above the national average, it is so much higher than crime rates in the rest of small-city America that it is likely to reflect a higher crime rate in the African population. If so, the effects of race differences in crime that apply to large cities could apply to small ones, particularly those of the 100,000–150,000 range. In the smaller cities and towns, the general considerations I discussed earlier would mitigate those effects.

## *Latin Small-City America*

To qualify as a part of Latin small-city America requires that Latins be at least 25 percent of the population and also be the largest minority in the town or city – a definition that includes almost 20 million Americans. In Latin small-city America, 47 percent of the population is Latin. The violent crime rate averages 231 per 100,000, which is 59 percent of the national rate.

This suggests that Latin crime rates are only modestly higher than European rates in small-city America. It's not necessarily true – mathematically, the crime rates in these towns and cities could be produced by very low European and Asian rates combined with a high Latin crime rate. But the two small cities with significant Latin populations among the thirteen I discussed in Chapter 4, Fort Lauderdale and Urbana, had Latin/European violent arrest ratios of just 1.3 and 1.2 respectively. This is consistent with the proposition that disproportionate Latin crime is usually a significant problem only in large cities. It will be important good news if this is confirmed by more city-level crime data by race.

---

Perhaps I have gone too far in minimizing the effects of race differences in crime in small-city America. The mitigating circumstances I have described are real, but as soon as a minority neighborhood becomes numerically and spatially large, the kind of effects that I described for big-city America are likely to kick in. Nonetheless, I think it is important to keep the distinction between big-city and small-city America in mind. Overall, the economic and social effects of race differences in crime are far greater in the former than in the latter.

# CHAPTER SIX

## SUMMING UP

Toward the end of his career, James Q. Wilson, who for decades was one of America's leading scholars of crime and policing, captured the essence of the problem posed by race and crime better than I can. His words are worth quoting at length:

> A central problem – perhaps *the* central problem – in improving the relationship between white and black Americans is the difference in racial crime rates. No matter how innocent or guilty a stranger may be, he carries with him in public the burdens or benefits of his group identity....
>
> ... When whites walk down the street, they are more nervous when they encounter a black man than when they encounter a white one. When blacks walk down the street, they are more likely than whites to be stopped and questioned by a police officer. It is important, of course, for whites to know that a chance encounter with a black creates little risk and for police officers to know that they should have more criteria than just skin color to decide who is worth questioning. Many whites and many police officers know this, but in spite of what people know, the racial tension persists. Countless white pedestrians have been worried by the sight of a young black male, and countless innocent black men have had their cars stopped or their walk interrupted by a suspicious cop. White pedestrians may be embarrassed by their own caution; certainly black pedestrians are upset by unwarranted police intrusions....
>
> ... Whites are fearful of living amid large numbers of blacks and of sending their children to predominately black schools. Blacks interpret the way

they are treated on the streets by white strangers and by police officers as a sign that they can never make much social progress. "No matter what I do, I can never be regarded as innocent," many embittered black men will say. "I cannot hail a cab as easily as a white, and I will be stopped and questioned by the police more than any white. Integration is a joke."

Every statement in that passage is as factually correct today as when Wilson wrote it in 2000. There is no reason to think they will stop being factually correct in the foreseeable future. The problem of race and crime requires us to accept two truths at the same time:

In any random encounter between two individuals of different races, whatever those races may be, the chance of any sort of violence is so small that any race differences in the probabilities of violence can be ignored.

The differences in the group rates of violence are real and large, and it is human nature, not racism, to take precautions accordingly.

## CHAPTER SEVEN

# If We Don't Face Reality

WE HAVE COME to the end of the facts I set out to present and, with it, the end of the material that led me to use *European*, *African*, and *Latin* as more detached labels than *White*, *Black*, and *Latino*. We are now back in the midst of political and cultural issues, and the semantic baggage that the customary labels carry is an integral part of the discussion.

I have many opinions about what policies we should pursue in dealing with the facts I have presented, but others can recognize the same facts and come to quite different opinions. I will be satisfied if this book accomplishes two things, both of which are within the realm of possibility.

First, I want *Facing Reality* to open a space for policy analysts to incorporate race differences into their analyses. Here are some examples of how I hope my colleagues can approach their work without fearing for their professional lives:

If you are researching the ways in which Black and Latino children are shortchanged by urban public education, make your case with the abundant evidence that is out there, but don't assume that successful reforms must raise test scores. Use other measures of success. Use the cognitive ability of students as an important independent variable that the design of effective reforms needs to take into account.

If you are researching racial discrimination in the job market, recognize that controlling for educational attainment isn't good enough (recall the data about the educational pipeline). Control for IQ as well.

If you are researching social mobility, take advantage of the mammoth databases that have been assembled on the importance of neighborhood factors, but supplement those analyses with information on cognitive ability. Without it, your inferences could be completely wrong.

If you are researching racist behavior by police, present the facts about police misconduct, but take into account that Black and Latino neighborhoods in big cities usually present a much more dangerous environment for police than White and Asian neighborhoods do. Develop policy recommendations that are consistent with that reality.

If you are researching the problems of the Black or Latino inner city, put the debilitating effects of crime on the same level of importance as poverty, drug use, bad schools, and family breakdown. Take a hard look at what happened to crime rates and policing in the most disadvantaged neighborhoods in the aftermath of the protests in the summer of 2020.

I could offer similar examples for research on other policy questions, such as the effects of income inequality, the efficacy of preschool and jobs programs, the causes of residential segregation, the voting behavior of the working class – take your choice. Research results on any domestic policy issue involving more than one race are seldom valid unless race differences in cognitive ability and crime are taken into account. I don't ask for much. I will be gratified if researchers are buffered from accusations of racism because they entered IQ scores as an independent variable in a regression equation.

But I hope for more. Conservatives have been grumbling about the lack of ideological diversity on campuses for decades, and they have had reason to, but it's time for conservative scholars to make common cause with their liberal colleagues. The new ideologues of the far left are akin to the Red Guards of Mao's Great Proletarian Cultural Revolution of the 1960s, and they are coming for all of us. The comparison is not overblown – not when students demand that an art professor at Skidmore be fired for briefly watching a "Back the Blue" demonstration and successfully intimidate other students into dropping his classes; not when the University of Southern California places a professor on leave after student protests because he used a common Chinese term that sounds something like the *n*-word; not when a Yale lecturer is subjected to ugly demonstrations over an email suggesting that Yale students should be allowed to make their own decisions about Halloween costumes.

These examples would be laughable if they didn't illustrate a mindset that is at war with the university's function. Over the last decade, on many campuses, the idea that a scholar's obligation is to search for the truth has become disreputable – seen as only a cover for scholarship that is racist, sexist, or heteronormative. Scholars are criticized not for the quality of their work but for its failure to advance the cause of social justice. Work seen as hostile to that cause is met with calls for the scholar's dismissal.

The result is widespread self-censorship in the social sciences that now extends to biology and medicine. Advances in neuroscience and genetics have already opened up the exploration of questions involving race, gender, and class that were previously closed. But in the eyes of the new Red Guards, such research is bound to be pernicious. After all, everyone knows that race is a social construct. Gender is a social construct. Socioeconomic class is a function of privilege. Research that says otherwise is pseudoscience. Having spent three years exploring research findings in these areas, I can report that intrepid neuroscientists and geneticists are doing important and valuable work. But I also know that some of those same scholars fear for their careers and have decided to cancel projects because they will attract too much hostile fire.

The most inexcusable effects of the ideological straitjacket on permissible work involve medicine. It is known without question that races sometimes have different genetic vulnerabilities to diseases or disabilities and sometimes respond differently to treatment regimens. The same is true of men and women. Researchers ought to be proceeding energetically to identify those differences and shape medical practices accordingly. Once again, valuable work is in fact being done, but it is not nearly as rapid or productive as it would be if the researchers weren't forced to engage in defensive precautions against the new Red Guards.

The second semirealistic goal I set for *Facing Reality* is to make life a little easier for journalists who are being attacked by their colleagues for lack of ideological purity. "We're all terrified of our staffs," an executive at a major news outlet observed to me recently. He was referring to younger staff, often twenty-somethings, often graduates of elite schools, who are committed to the new orthodoxy, certain of their righteousness, and who make life difficult for staff members who are guilty of wrongthink.

Recent examples of victims as I write include James Bennet, formerly opinion editor at the *New York Times*, who was forced out of his position because he authorized an op-ed column by Senator Tom Cotton that offended the *Times*'s "woke" staff. Other examples are the decisions of Andrew Sullivan (*New York* magazine), Matthew Yglesias (*Vox*), Bari Weiss (*New York Times*), and Glenn Greenwald (*The Intercept*) to leave their positions because of the ideological conformity that was demanded of them. Those are only the best-known examples – symptoms of a deeper fear among many more who cannot risk losing their jobs. Bari Weiss described the situation in her resignation letter: "If a person's ideology is in keeping with the new orthodoxy, they and their work remain unscrutinized. Everyone else lives in fear of the digital thunderdome."

The new Red Guards have been successful when it comes to racial issues because pushback from the victims has been so feeble. The pushback has been so feeble in part because no one has been willing to say, "The systemically racist America you portray doesn't exist." Perhaps publicizing the two truths about race will make it easier for journalists accused of heresy to be able to say, "It's more complicated than you acknowledge." Perhaps it will make editors a little more willing to publish heretical stories.

My thought is that the new Red Guards are garden-variety bullies, with the bully's underlying cowardice. They are happy when they are part of a mob, when they can threaten and harangue without fear of contradiction. But most of them have adopted their radicalism without much thought. They have strident passions but brittle convictions. They aren't really prepared to *argue* for their positions. Even a little contradiction bothers them and will cause many of them to choose easier targets. Such is my hope.

My own overarching position is that racism persists in America, but it persists in spite of the American system and its institutions, not because of them. Many of the *problems* are systemic, but they will not be solved by going after racism. They will be solved, or ameliorated, by going after systemic educational problems, systemic law enforcement problems, systemic employment problems. Those problems are exacerbated by individual racism. The racism is not systemic.

So much for the practical effects of *Facing Reality* that I like to think are within the realm of possibility. A much more important topic remains. I began this book by invoking a looming disaster if we don't face reality. It is time to explain the disaster I have in mind. It's pretty simple:

Identity politics is an existential threat to the American experiment.

If working-class and middle-class Whites adopt identity politics, disaster follows.

## WHY IDENTITY POLITICS IS AN EXISTENTIAL THREAT TO THE AMERICAN EXPERIMENT

The American experiment is fragile. It has always been fragile and always will be fragile because it is so extremely unnatural. "Unnatural" in this context means in conflict with human nature.

### *The Garden*

Jonah Goldberg has described the fragility of the American system by comparing it to a garden hacked out of a tropical jungle. A garden surrounded by jungle is unnatural. The gardeners must tend it with unremitting care lest the jungle return.

Treating our fellow human beings as individuals instead of treating them as members of groups is unnatural. Our brains evolved to think of people as members of groups; to trust and care for people who are like us and to be suspicious of people who are unlike us. Those traits had great survival value for human beings throughout millions of years of evolution. People who were trusting of outsiders were less likely to pass on their genes than people who were suspicious of them. People who were loyal to their tribe were more likely to pass on their genes than people who stood apart.

The invention of agriculture and the consequent rise of complex societies exposed another aspect of human nature that had enjoyed less scope for expression in hunter-gatherer bands: acquisitiveness, whether of money, status, or power. Whatever its evolutionary roots may be, the empirical consistency of human acquisitiveness over the eons is impressive. The open-ended desire for more money, status, or power has been natural; to voluntarily limit one's wealth, status, or power has been unnatural.

The combination of acquisitiveness and loyalty to the interests of one's own group (be it defined by ethnicity or class) shaped human governments for the subsequent ten thousand years. The natural form of government was hierarchical, run by a dominant group that arranged affairs to its benefit and oppressed outsiders to a lesser or greater degree, usually greater. The rare attempts to try any other form of government were unstable and short-lived. The American founders' idealism lay in their belief that an alternative was possible. Their genius was to design a system with multiple safeguards against the forces that had made previous attempts self-destruct.

America proved that a durable alternative to the natural form of government was possible – a constitutional republic combined with carefully circumscribed democracy. The idea behind that alternative eventually spread around the world, but neither the United States nor any other country that has made it work has ever been out of danger. If we decide that our system for tending the garden needs to be replaced, and if the replacement should prove to be even slightly less devoted to keeping nature at bay, the garden will be reclaimed by jungle within a few decades.

The introduction of identity politics into that carefully crafted constitutional system does not simply distract us from warding off the jungle. It *is* the jungle, the primitive sense of "us against them" pressing in upon the garden. It not only permits but insists that the power of the state be used to reward favored groups at the expense of everyone else. That view of power is the defining characteristic of the natural form of government that humankind endured until the miracle at Philadelphia in 1787.

### The Peril of Using Outliers to Dismiss Differences in Means

Many of you were taught about the fragility of democracy in your first high school civics course and don't have difficulty accepting the analogy of the garden. But I am sure that many of you also have come to this page unconvinced that the facts of group differences are as important as I have claimed. I suggest that a reason for such a reaction is grounded in another aspect of human nature: the impulse to generalize from our own experience even when we know intellectually that our experience is not representative.

I project that reaction onto you (which of course you may not have had) based on my experience in the quarter century since *The Bell Curve* appeared. Too many of the

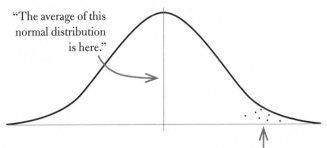

"The average of this normal distribution is here."

"Well then, how do you explain the fact that THESE points exist?! YOU CAN'T" conversations I've had resemble one that I recently saw depicted on the Internet, as shown here.

The experience of most White readers of this book – disproportionately college-educated and upper middle class – includes many Black and Latino acquaintances who correspond to the dots on the right-hand tail of that graphic. For example, suppose that your personal experience has consisted of life as a White in an upper-middle-class American suburb. Your Black, Latino, and Asian neighbors have been as smart, engaging, and helpful as your White neighbors. The bell curve of your personal experience does not involve mean differences in cognitive ability or crime rates. It is natural to think your experience invalidates the data about group differences in means. The mind insists on generalizing. *But when mean differences between groups are real, it is absolutely essential to resist generalizing; it is essential to accept the reality of documented group differences but to insist on thinking of and treating every person as an individual.*

Why resist generalizing? After all, even if you're technically "making a mistake" with your generalization, it's on the side of generosity and optimism. How could that be bad? The answer is that if it's okay for you to do it, it's okay for everyone else to do it. That way lies unrestrained racism.

Suppose that instead of living in an upper-middle-class suburb you are a White living in a multiracial working-class or middle-class neighborhood in a megalopolis. The great majority of crimes are committed by minorities. Most of the children in the bottom of the class in your child's school are minorities. These observations are not the products of a racist imagination. They are the facts of your lived experience. There are exceptions, to be sure – your daughter's super-smart minority classmate, the minority couple down the street who provide loving care for foster children, the minority cop you watched deftly defuse an escalating confrontation. But your lived experience tells you that these are not typical. Is it okay for you to generalize that minorities are criminal and dumb? Obviously not. The obviously correct answer is that a difference in means exists, but that we must insist on treating people as individuals.

If you agree that it's wrong for Whites living in a multiracial working-class or middle-class neighborhood to generalize from their experience but think that it's still okay for Whites in an affluent neighborhood to do so, then I ask that you take two other considerations on board:

> Advocating double standards for people on top and everyone else is a bad idea.

> A lot more Whites live in working-class and middle-class neighborhoods than in affluent ones.

These two considerations are politically pragmatic. The elites who run the country would arouse much less hostility if they kept both of them at the front of their minds.

The truly grave danger of refusing to confront race differences in means is that it leads in a straight line to thinking that the only legitimate evidence of a nonracist society is equal outcomes. It appears that the Biden administration already accepts that logic. If that's what the people in power truly believe, and if those equal outcomes continue to elude them, the logical conclusion is that the state must force equal outcomes by whatever means necessary. Once the state is granted the power to engineer equal outcomes by dispensing opportunities preferentially and freedoms selectively, it will be one group versus another, "us" against "them." The garden will give way to jungle.

People on the left understand the danger to the nation posed by those on the far right who applaud violence and racism. People on the right understand the danger to the nation posed by those on the far left who insist that Whites are irredeemably racist. But we need everyone to understand that what keeps us all safe is the state's impartiality.

## If Whites Adopt Identity Politics, Disaster Follows

Preferential racial policies have been eroding the nation's commitment to impartiality for decades. Identity politics accelerated that erosion. The threatening new development is that Whites increasingly agree that identity politics is the way to go.

In retrospect, President Obama's eight years in office look like a prolonged inflection point for race relations. In 2001, Gallup's pollsters began asking the question, "Would you say relations between whites and blacks are very good, somewhat good, somewhat bad, or very bad." Seventy percent of Whites and 62 percent of Blacks answered that they were either "very good" or "somewhat good." When Barack Obama was elected in 2008, those numbers were almost the same: 70 percent and 61 percent respectively. During his first term, they improved slightly, standing at 72 percent and 66 percent in 2013.

When Gallup next asked the question about race relations just two years later, the number for Whites who thought that relations were "very good" or "somewhat good" had fallen off a cliff, from 71 to 45 percent. The Black number had dropped from 66 to 51 percent. During the Trump years, the White number stabilized – it was 46 percent in 2020 – but the Black number fell to 36 percent. In just seven years, Americans' perceptions of race relations had gone from solidly optimistic to solidly pessimistic.

During that time, race also became more closely tied to the nation's political divisions. You have probably seen electoral maps similar to the pair in Figure 3 in the insert, but it's worth your time to contemplate them in light of the material I've presented. They are the 1996 and 2016 presidential electoral maps. The units in the maps are counties. The darker the color (blue or red), the bigger the margin for the Democratic or Republican candidate.

When Bill Clinton won a second term in 1996, the electoral map of counties was a mix of red and blue shades, mostly pale on both sides. The deep red counties were confined largely to Bob Dole's home state, Kansas, and its neighbors. The blue counties showed no obvious correspondence with racial composition – some of them were in counties with large minority populations, but even more of them were in counties where Whites constituted more than 80 percent of the population.

Just four years later, the county map of the 2000 election already showed the basic shape of the coming polarization – blue on the coasts, red in between, but less starkly divided and with mostly pale shades of red and blue. By 2016, the interior of the country was overwhelmingly red. The remaining blue counties in the Mountain West were those with large populations of Amerindians. The blue counties in the South were ones with large Black populations. The blue counties in the Southwest were ones with large Latino populations. Outside big-city America, White America had become landslide-red Republican.

Much of that change had nothing to do with race relations or identity politics, but with the alienation of middle-class and working-class Whites from the coastal elites. I have written about that alienation at length. But if identity politics did not start the change, it had become part it. Compare the two electoral maps in Figure 3 with the one in Figure 4. It is also based on counties. Red counties are ones in which at least 50 percent of the population is White. The darker the red, the higher the percentage. Blue counties are ones in which Whites are not a majority. The darker the blue, the higher the percentage of minorities.

This map looks strikingly similar to the map of the 2016 presidential election. The main difference is that light pink counties in this race-based map are often dark red counties in the election map. The polarization continued during the Trump years. The 2020 map is almost indistinguishable from the 2016 map despite the different electoral outcome.

Perhaps the deepening polarization would have continued just because of the alienation between elites on the coasts and the people who live everywhere else. It is also plausible that the alienation between Blacks and Whites played a role. Purely on grounds of expediency, the rhetoric about White privilege and systemic racism coming from Black opinion leaders has always seemed self-defeating. Blacks, constituting 13 percent of the population, are telling Whites, 60 percent of the population, that they are racist, bad people, the cause of Blacks' problems, and they had better change their ways or else. Right or wrong, that rhetoric has been guaranteed to produce backlash by some portion of the 60 percent against the 13 percent. So far, this effect has been masked because the strategy has worked so well with White elites. Ordinarily, you can't insult people into agreeing with you, but White guilt is a real thing. In the summer of 2020, many White college students and young adults agreed that they had sinned, even though they hadn't realized it until now, and joined in Black Lives Matter marches. The *New York Times*, the *Washington Post*, NPR, PBS, CBS, NBC, ABC, CNN, and MSNBC gave sympathetic coverage to the protests and, to varying degrees, downplayed the riots and looting.

Meanwhile, many middle-class and working-class Whites have not been insulted into agreement. They're just insulted, and to their minds unfairly insulted. I'm not talking about White nationalists and White supremacists –

their numbers are relatively small. My concern is the extremely large majority of middle-class and working-class Whites who don't think of themselves as racists and have not behaved as racists.

Tens of millions of these people live in towns that have few Black or Latino residents, and racial issues haven't impinged on their lives. They don't understand why they are being accused of racism. Still other tens of millions live in large cities where racial problems have been real, but they see themselves as having treated Black and Latino neighbors and coworkers with friendship and respect. They believe that everyone has a God-given right to be treated equally. Now all of them are being told that they are privileged and racist, and they are asking on what grounds. They are living ordinary lives, with average incomes, working hard to make ends meet. They can't see what "White privilege" they have ever enjoyed. Some are fed up and ready to push back.

How widespread might the backlash be? It is one of those topics that the elite media has been unable to investigate more than superficially. But it seems beyond dispute that a growing number of Whites are disposed to adopt identity politics – to become a racial interest group in the same way that Blacks and Latinos are racial interest groups.

The question asks itself: If a minority consisting of 13 percent of the population can generate as much political energy and solidarity as America's Blacks have, what happens when a large proportion of the 60 percent of the population that is White begins to use the same playbook? I could spin out a variety of scenarios, but I don't have confidence in any of them. I am certain of only two things.

First, the White backlash is occurring in the context of long-term erosion in the federal government's legitimacy. Since 1958, the Gallup polling organization has periodically asked Americans how much they trust the federal government to do what is right. In 1958, 73 percent said "always" or "most of the time." Trust hit its high point in 1964, when that figure stood at 77 percent. Then it began to fall. By 1980, only 27 percent trusted the government to do what is right. That percentage rebounded to the low 40s during the Reagan years, then fell to a new low, 19 percent, in 1994. It rebounded again, hitting a short-lived high of 54 percent just after 9/11. Then it plunged again, hitting another new low, 15 percent, in 2011. It has been in the 15–20 percent range ever since. A government that is distrusted by more than 80 percent of the citizens has a bipartisan legitimacy problem.

When a government loses legitimacy, it loses some of the allegiance of its citizens. That weakened allegiance means, among other things, a greater willingness to ignore the law. The federal government has enacted thousands of laws and regulations. Many of them apply to every family and every business in the nation. They cannot possibly be enforced by the police or courts without almost universal voluntary compliance. When a government is seen as legitimate, most citizens voluntarily comply because it is part of being a citizen; they don't agree with every law and regulation, but they believe it is their duty as citizens to respect them. When instead people see laws and regulations as products of the illegitimate use of power, the sense of obligation fades.

Events since the summer of 2020 make me think it is too late to talk about *if* Whites adopt identity politics. Many already have. That's the parsimonious way to interpret the red-blue divisions over wearing masks, the widespread belief in red states that the 2020 election was stolen, and the rage that resulted in the invasion of the U.S. Capitol on January 6, 2021. This is all evidence that the federal government has lost its legitimacy in the eyes of many Whites. If that reaction spreads, the continued ability of the federal government to enforce its edicts in the reddest portions of the nation will be thrown into question. The prospect of legal secession may be remote, but the prospect of reduced governability from Washington is not.

The second thing of which I am certain is that Donald Trump's election and the lessons of his term in office changed the parameters of what is politically possible in America. Someone can win the presidency without having been a governor, a senator, or a general. Someone can win it without any experience in public service at all and without any other relevant experience. Someone can win with a populist agenda. Someone can govern without observing any of the norms of presidential behavior.

Those lessons have not been lost on the politically ambitious of either the left or the right. All over the country, people at the outset of their political careers see a new set of possibilities. They include many who are as indifferent to precedent and self-restraint as Donald Trump was and who are more serious students of the uses of power than Trump was. It is increasingly possible that, the next time around, someone who is far more adept than Donald Trump can govern by ignoring inconvenient portions of the Constitution.

## THE SOLUTION THAT IS NOT WITHIN OUR GRASP

I will briefly state my own sense of a root policy problem and the required solution. The solution is not politically within the realm of possibility, but I think it is useful to put it on the table.

*The problem.* The phrase "affirmative action" originally referred to initiatives by colleges and corporations to seek out qualified Blacks who were being overlooked for educational and job opportunities. It was a needed policy in the mid-1960s and legally innocuous. But it soon morphed into aggressive affirmative action, meaning government-sponsored preferential treatment in determining who gets the educations and the jobs.

Working-class and middle-class Whites who now see themselves as second-class citizens in the eyes of the government aren't making it up. Of course they are not enduring anything remotely comparable to the legally sanctioned inequalities that Blacks faced until 1964. But they are now told – by government officials, college administrators, and corporate human resources managers – to get in line behind minority applicants for admission to elite colleges and for employment and promotion in attractive white-collar jobs. Well-to-do Whites can find ways to circumvent this problem, but working-class and middle-class Whites cannot. It has long been my view, first expressed in these words long ago, that aggressive affirmative action is a poison leaking into the American experiment. We are now dealing with nearly sixty years of accumulated toxin. It is not the only cause of the present crisis, but it is a central one.

It also has a side effect that I have never seen or heard discussed in public. Aggressive affirmative action is practiced most sweepingly for government jobs at all levels. At the city level, it affects the selection and promotion of police, prosecutors, public defenders, correctional officers, personnel in the social welfare bureaucracies, health-care workers on the public payroll, and K–12 teachers in the public schools.

The presence of incompetent or marginally competent people in those jobs is only occasionally important to members of America's upper middle class. Many of them live in places where affirmative action is not an issue because so few minorities live in their communities. For those who live in multiracial cities, incompetent police and prosecutors can be a problem. Incompetent teachers have driven many of them from the public schools. But upper-middle-class families in urban areas don't have much to do with public defenders, correctional officers, or personnel in the social welfare bureaucracies. The burden of the substandard government services produced by aggressive affirmative action is borne overwhelmingly by America's poorest and most vulnerable populations. It's a side effect, not the central reason that aggressive affirmative action is destructive. But it should be more widely recognized.

*The solution.* Eliminate all forms of government-sponsored preferential treatment by race. It is not within any government's power to force racial harmony on its citizens, but it is within the government's power to strip away the legal and administrative incentives and requirements for preferential treatment according to race. Limit antidiscrimination law and its enforcement to behaviors that would be unacceptable regardless of race – behaviors, not statistical evidence of disparate impact.

Left and right will still be free to argue about the size and benefits of the welfare state. They will be free to argue about how much the government should limit the rights of employers in hiring, firing, and promotions. Some laws and regulations will still need to be expressed differentially because of sex or physical disabilities. But when it comes to race, all Americans are to be treated impartially under the government's administrative rules and to have equal standing before the law.

## THE PARTIAL SOLUTION THAT IS WITHIN OUR GRASP

Bernard Bailyn, the great historian of America's Revolutionary era, liked to remind his fellow historians that they know how things turned out. The people who made the history didn't know how things would turn out, and you can't understand their thinking or actions without keeping that in mind.

I never felt the force of Bailyn's point until recently. When I first encountered arguments that we might be living through the last half of the 1850s all over again, I dismissed them as farfetched. But if I were to look back at the 1850s without Bailyn's caution in mind, I would probably think that the people running the country then were inexplicably myopic. So few who were living through those years realized the enormity of what was happening. They knew that North and South were badly divided. Some of them saw that secession was a possibility – but if it came, surely it wouldn't mean a war. Or if it came to war, surely it would be a perfunctory war and soon settled. Only a handful foresaw catastrophe.

It's easy to think that the American elites of the 1850s should have seen it coming, but that's because we know how it turned out. We don't know how the present crisis is going to turn out. I am now slower to assume that we will avoid catastrophe. I'm gloomier about just how awful things might get very quickly.

I can think of only one measure that is practicable and might make a significant difference: To restore the American creed as the ideal shared by a consensus of the electorate. I think it could happen because I am confident that the principles of the creed are still attractive to a large majority of Americans of both parties, however much we may disagree about the rightness of specific policies.

If this is true, then why are we allowing the voices that say we should treat people as groups to drown out everyone else? Why are we allowing the few who sneer at the melting pot and the goal of colorblindness to shout down the many who still believe in these ideals? Why are so many of us afraid to say that treating people as individuals who are equal under the law is intrinsic to a free society?

My practical suggestion is that the people who still embrace the American creed start declaring it out loud. As simple as that.

The leaders of the Democratic Party, starting with President Biden, are indispensable. I don't expect him to renounce policies involving racial preferences. He just needs to treat them as pragmatic measures to deal with residual racism, endorse equality before the law as the ultimate goal, and disassociate himself from the rhetoric of systemic racism. It would represent a big improvement. So would such statements coming from Democratic leaders in the House and the Senate and from liberal opinion leaders in the media and academia.

For their part, leaders of the Republican Party must stop posturing as the guardians of true Americanism and instead say out loud in front of cameras and microphones that the people who love this country have always been on both sides of the political spectrum and still are today. As simple as that.

If both of those things were to happen, it would be much easier for people on the center left and the center right to say out loud to friends and relatives that they repudiate the extremists on their own side. It would be much easier for Blacks and Latinos to say out loud to friends and relatives that they love America.

The return to an embrace of the American creed must be a celebration of America's original ideal of equality under the law. The good news is that there is indeed much for us to celebrate in common. When we turn away from the television news and social media feeds on our glowing digital rectangles and focus instead on our actual day-to-day interactions with Americans who don't look like us, we see abundant evidence that the optimism and good will that have been hallmarks of Americanism remain essentially intact at the micro level, though perhaps a little frazzled.

I am not hoping for full-fledged national reconciliation. Partisan disagreements, including bitter ones, are as American as apple pie, and they will continue. But pride in being an American is also as American as apple pie – not pride in America's perfection, but pride in an ideal that we originated, that no other nation has improved upon, and that we as a nation have done so much to realize. Bearing witness to our true faith and allegiance in the American creed is something within our power to do. It is not enough to bring us all the way back. It would be a good start.

———

In 1782, the founders of the newly independent United States chose the motto *novus ordo seclorum* – "a new order of the ages" – to inscribe on the Great Seal. They were right to do so. The creation of a nation dedicated to the proposition that every individual has the same rights to liberty and the same innate human dignity as everyone else was an unprecedented world-historical event. But I fear that we are nearing a point of no return. We must reaffirm the American creed explicitly and quickly, or this country will become just another big power like other big powers, governed with all the historic oppressions that America tried to cast off. In that event, we will not only have sacrificed our heritage. We will lose foundational freedoms and jeopardize even the rule of law. All of us who think that this catastrophe has become a real possibility are obligated to do whatever we can do to turn the nation around. For me, "whatever we can do" has been to write this book.

# Notes

The endnotes that follow are only a fraction of the material that is available to the curious at encounterbooks.com/books/facing-reality. The notes I include here are restricted to material that readers might need to answer their most immediate questions. Some of that material cites specific sources, but most of the documentation of sources in this book is reserved for the online documentation.

*Facing Reality* is not a formally academic text, so I have taken the liberty of streamlining my citation format to fit the way scholars actually do their research these days. They no longer acquire a specific volume of a technical journal from the library stacks and look up an article by using the issue number and page numbers in the citation. They type the title of the article (even a portion of it is usually enough) and perhaps the surname of one of the authors into their Internet browser and hit "return." So I have used an abbreviated form of article citation, with everything needed to find the source. I include the page number for citations of direct quotes. In the case of Internet sources, I avoid linking to a specific page because they so quickly go out of date, instead trying to give you a link that will get you to the correct website with enough additional information to let you search for the appropriate page.

## CHAPTER 1: THE AMERICAN CREED IMPERILED

1. Samuel P. Huntington's *Who Are We? The Challenges to America's National Identity* (2005), a brilliant book, is the best recent source about the American creed. The quotation is taken from p. 46. For descriptions of how thoroughly the American creed (though not yet called that) permeated life in the early nineteenth century, see Francis Grund, *The Americans in Their Moral, Social, and Political Relations* (1837) and, of course, Alexis de Tocqueville, *Democracy in America* (1838). For a description of how the creed persisted at the end of the nineteenth century, see a two-volume study, James Bryce, *The American Commonwealth* (1903). Bryce, a leading British scholar of American society at the time, reflected on "certain dogmas or maxims which are in so far fundamental that ... one usually strikes upon them when sinking a shaft, so to speak, in an American mind" – dogmas and maxims that amounted to the American creed (pp. 536–37).

   During World War I, the U.S. House of Representatives passed a resolution titled "The American's Creed" written by William Tyler Page. It conveys elements of the creed as I describe it but is by no means an official definition. To my knowledge, there isn't one.

## CHAPTER 2: MULTIRACIAL AMERICA

1. In 2001, the Gallup polling organization found that the average American estimated that 32 percent of the population was Black. The correct answer was 12.3 percent. The same poll found that the average American thought that 29 percent of the population was Latino. The correct answer was 12.5 percent. Joseph Carroll, "Public Overestimates U.S. Black and Latino Populations," Gallup News (June 4, 2001).

   Gallup has not asked those questions since 2001, but a 2013 survey by the Center for American Progress indicated that the American public still overestimated the size of minority populations. Most Blacks and Latinos thought that minorities combined already made up half the population or more, while non-Latino Whites estimated that minorities were 48 percent of the population. Only Asians (who gave an estimate of 43 percent) were even close to the correct answer, which in 2013 was 37 percent. See Ruy Teixeira and John Halpin, "Building an All-In Nation: A View from the American Public," Center for American Progress (October 22, 2013).

2. You may have a larger question about the substitution of *European* for *White*: Is it still accurate, given recent immigration of peoples from North Africa and the Middle East who in the old terminology are classified as Caucasian? Part of the answer lies in the 23andMe results showing that self-identified Whites had 98.6 percent European ancestry. Additional evidence may be found in the combined ACS surveys for 2014–2018, which reveal that 95.1 percent of non-Latin Whites who answered the "Ancestry 1" question specified a European ancestry while only 1.6 percent gave a North African or Middle Eastern ancestry. *Europeans* seems reasonable as a way of identifying the way that the overwhelming majority of non-Latin Whites think of themselves.

3. It is possible that the percentage of Latins in 1960 is understated. The limited information in the 1960 census is frustrating. There is no "Latino" category either as part of the "What race are you?" question or as a separate "What ethnicity are you?" question. A separate table shows country of birth for the foreign-born, reporting that 1,735,992 people were born in Mexico, but the numbers in the table for race are inconsistent with the numbers in the table on country of birth for the foreign-born. But my estimate could be too low by half and we would still be talking about only 3 or 4 percent of the population who were not European or African.

### CHAPTER 3: RACE DIFFERENCES IN COGNITIVE ABILITY

1. If you want to know the whole story and are reasonably knowledgeable about statistics, go to Arthur Jensen's magisterial *The g Factor: The Science of Mental Ability* (1998). For more recent and readable discussions of what IQ tests measure, the thorough version is Russell Warne, *In the Know: Debunking 35 Myths about Human Intelligence* (2020). A short, breezy, but scientifically accurate account is Stuart Ritchie, *Intelligence: All That Matters* (2015).

2. The importance of self-esteem, so enthusiastically assumed by educators from the 1970s through the end of the century, flunked empirical attempts to demonstrate its causal role in academic performance or other achievements. A single comprehensive review article dismantled self-esteem's reputation among scholars, partly because of its massive documentation and partly because the lead

author had previously been an open advocate of the importance of self-esteem. See Roy Baumeister, Jennifer D. Campbell, Joachim I. Krueger, and Kathleen D. Vohs, "Does High Self-Esteem Cause Better Performance, Interpersonal Success, Happiness, or Healthier Lifestyles?" *Psychological Science in the Public Interest* (2003).

"Stereotype threat" enjoyed a similar vogue from 1995 through the next twenty years. The concept was introduced by Claude M. Steele and Joshua Aronson in "Stereotype Threat and the Intellectual Test Performance of African Americans," *Journal of Personality and Social Psychology* (1995). It was seized upon so uncritically that by 2003, just eight years after its debut, it was already covered in two-thirds of introductory psychology textbooks.

Since 2015, its reputation has been battered by a series of failures to replicate the effects seen in early studies and by evidence of "publication bias" – the tendency of scholars to fail to publish negative results. Two of the most rigorous critiques leave little room for the advocates of stereotype threat to make their case: Paulette C. Flore and Jelte M. Wicherts, "Does Stereotype Threat Influence Performance of Girls in Stereotyped Domains? A Meta-Analysis," *Journal of School Psychology* (2015); and Oren Shewach, Paul R. Sackett, and Sander Quint, "Stereotype Threat Effects in Settings with Features Likely Versus Unlikely in Operational Test Settings: A Meta-Analysis," *Journal of Applied Psychology* (2019). The former, coauthored by one the world's most highly regarded quantitative social science methodologists (Jelte Wicherts), concluded that "based on the small average effect size in our meta-analysis, which is most likely inflated due to publication bias, we would not feel confident to proclaim that stereotype manipulations will harm mathematic performance of girls in a systematic way." (p. 41). The latter article, written by a team of psychologists at the University of Minnesota, concluded, "Based on the result of the focal analysis, operational and motivational subsets, and publication bias analyses, we conclude that the burden of proof shifts back to those that claim that stereotype threat exerts a substantial effect on standardized test takers." (p. 1529).

3. If you have come to *Facing Reality* thinking that Stephen J. Gould demolished the concept of *g* forty years ago with *The Mismeasure of Man* (1981), you should know that the scientific consensus about that book is that Gould had attacked psychometrics as it stood in the 1930s and systematically misrepresented psychometrics

as it stood when he was writing in the 1970s. See Arthur Jensen, "The Debunking of Scientific Fossils and Straw Persons," *Contemporary Education Review* (1982); Bernard D. Davis, "Neo-Lysenkoism, IQ, and the Press," *Public Interest* (1983); and John B. Carroll, "Reflections on Stephen Jay Gould's *The Mismeasure of Man* (1981): A Retrospective Review," *Intelligence* (1995). A 2019 analysis by a team of psychologists concluded as follows: "Given Gould's pervasively incorrect statements in *The Mismeasure of Man* about the Army Beta, factor analysis, the place of intelligence testing in the immigration debates of the 1920s, the biological basis for intelligence, and the questions regarding Gould's analysis of Morton's work, we wonder whether there is *any* section of *The Mismeasure of Man* that is factually accurate." Russell T. Warne, Jared Z. Burton, Aisa Gibbons, and Daniel A. Melendez, "Stephen Jay Gould's Analysis of the Army Beta Test in The Mismeasure of Man: Distortions and Misconceptions Regarding a Pioneering Mental Test," *Journal of Intelligence* (2019), p. 18. Emphasis in the original.

Or you may think that Nassim Taleb has more recently proved that, as he titled his article, "IQ is largely a pseudoscientific swindle," medium.com/incerto (January 1, 2019). Several responses are available on the Internet. One of the first but also most direct is Sean Last, "Nassim Taleb on IQ," archive.ph/PCvgk (January 8, 2019). Jonatan Pallesen gives a highly technical response in "Taleb is wrong about IQ," jsmp.dk (June 15, 2019), but that's unavoidable in dealing with some of Taleb's statistical assertions. James Thompson has an accessible series of articles about Taleb's arguments. The first three are "Swanning About: Fooled by Algebra?" "In the Wake of the Swan," and "The Intelligent Investor," all available at the *Unz Review* (unz.com).

4. Howard Gardner's theory of multiple intelligences is orthogonal to the psychometrics literature. His presentation of the theory in *Frames of Mind: The Theory of Multiple Intelligences* (1983) is a fascinating discussion of human talents, but he has never tried to prove statistically that his "intelligences" can be distinguished from *g* or from personality traits. Gardner offered this amusing and I think correct observation in a 2018 interview: "I have never been able to reconstruct when I made the fateful decision not to call these abilities, talents, or gifts, but rather to call them 'intelligences.' Because if I had called them anything else, I would not be well known in different corners of the world and journalists like you

wouldn't come to interview me. It was picking the word 'intelligence' and pluralizing it." Liz Mineo, " 'The Greatest Gift You Can Have Is a Good Education, One That Isn't Strictly Professional,' " *Harvard Gazette* (May 9, 2018).

5. The results from all the known studies of African intelligence through the 1950s are reported in Audrey M. Shuey, *The Testing of Negro Intelligence* (1966). The first large sample used to calculate African cognitive ability was assembled during World War I, when the U.S. Army used two IQ tests for incoming recruits, one designed for literate recruits and the other designed for illiterate or non-English-speaking recruits. Robert Yerkes found a European–African difference of 1.16 SDs, reported in John C. Loehlin, Gardner Lindzey, and J. N. Spuhler, *Race Differences in Intelligence* (1975), but little confidence can be attached to that number. Even a bad elementary education is associated with a substantial increase in cognitive ability over a population with no elementary education. As of World War I, 70 percent of all Blacks still lived in the rural South, where most African children got only the most rudimentary education or no education at all. There is reason to believe that this population was underrepresented among those draftees who reached the point of being administered the Army Alpha and Army Beta tests. See Jeanette Keith, *Rich Man's War, Poor Man's Fight: Race, Class, and Power in the Rural South During the First World War* (2004).

The caution with which one must approach the World War I data is accentuated by the data from World War II. The European–African difference on the Army General Classification Test for inductions in 1944–1945 has been put at 1.52 SDs (Loehlin, *Race Differences*). This represents the scores of men born from 1925 to 1927 and is very close to the 1.59 SD difference observed among the Woodcock-Johnson subjects born in the 1920s. See Charles Murray, "The Magnitude and Components of Change in the Black-White IQ Difference from 1920–1991: A Birth Cohort Analysis of the Woodcock-Johnson Standardizations," *Intelligence* (2007).

How could the European–African difference in cognitive ability have risen from 1.16 SDs to 1.52 SDs in 20 years? The simplest explanation is that the World War II testing produced a more accurate estimate of the European–African difference than did the World War I testing.

6. The phrase "*g*-loaded" traces its roots to the English psychologist

Charles Spearman's seminal 1904 article, "'General Intelligence,' Objectively Determined and Measured," in the *American Journal of Psychology*. Spearman observed that students' test scores across unrelated subjects were statistically correlated. His explanation was that the correlations reflected a general underlying mental ability, which he called *g* for *general*. The most powerful tool for measuring *g* is a statistical method called factor analysis. When the subtests in an IQ test battery are factor-analyzed, the first factor always explains a much larger proportion of the variation across the subtests than any other. That first factor is *g*. The *g-loading* of a subtest is its correlation with the overall measure of *g*. I sometimes use the phrase more loosely to signify a test that is a good measure of *g*, meaning that its correlation with the overall measure of *g* would be high if it were a subtest in an IQ test battery.

7. Scores on academic achievement tests are affected by the test taker's education – you can't score well on a reading comprehension test unless you know how to read. But reading tests such as the ones for the NAEP or the SAT don't ask how much the student has learned with questions (for example) about how *Middlemarch* fits into the history of the English novel. The tests present passages of text and ask about the meaning of those self-contained passages, which calls directly upon the test taker's ability to figure things out. The same principle applies to the NAEP math tests: the items are devised so that they presume only the math courses that are normally required of 4th-, 8th-, and 12th-graders. The test items require the students to figure out the answers from information contained in the items themselves. Composites of the major standardized tests of math and reading skills are thus *g*-loaded, but they don't provide as good a measure of *g* as a more comprehensive set of cognitive subtests.

8. The group differences are likely to increase as highly *g*-loaded tests are added because of another of Charles Spearman's hypotheses: the higher the *g*-loading of a subtest, the greater the size of group differences in IQ. The hypothesis has subsequently been confirmed through an extensive literature. See Arthur Jensen, *The* g *Factor: The Science of Mental Ability* (1998), pp. 369–402.

9. The proper method for combining separate measures depends on what you're trying to measure. Sometimes it is appropriate to add them (for example, if you are trying to measure a family's aggregate income you just add wages and dividend income); sometimes to

take the mean (for example, of judges' ratings in a gymnastics competition); and sometimes – as in the case of measuring cognitive ability – to add them after taking into account what they share. Verbal and mathematics ability are expressions of the same mental ability to some extent but also contribute independently to mental ability. The size of the add-on to a simple mean depends on the correlation between the two test scores. If the correlation were a perfect 1.0, the correct composite score would be the mean of the two scores because the two tests are imparting exactly the same information about mental ability. The lower the correlation between the tests, the more that each test is contributing independently to the measure of cognitive ability. As an empirical matter, correlations of reading and math tests in different studies cluster in the .60 to .75 range, which means a modest but nontrivial add-on to the mean.

10. Think of the standard deviation (SD) as a measure of spread-outness in a distribution of scores. If you're measuring height and your sample consists of five-year-olds, the SD of height is going to be compressed into a range of a few inches. If your sample includes everyone from infants to adults, the spread of heights will include everyone from newborns to NBA players, and the SD will be much larger.

The equation for computing a standard deviation of a population is this:

$$S = \sqrt{\frac{\Sigma(X-\overline{X})^2}{N}}$$

where $S$ = the standard deviation of a sample
$\Sigma$ means "sum of"
$X$ = each value in the data set
$\overline{X}$ = mean of all values in the data set
$N$ = number of values in the data set

Just as the average of a set of numbers is its sum divided by the number of numbers, the standard deviation represents the average *difference* between the numbers in a set and the mean for that set. That's not precisely correct – note the need to square the differences and eventually take the square root – but it's a convenient way to remember the basic concept.

11. Any set of scores can be converted to *z*-scores, but a normal distribution is necessary for accurate conversion of *z*-scores to percentiles.

12. Recent years have seen much work on establishing IQ estimates for countries around the world, but that is no help in trying to estimate ethnic subgroup means for U.S. populations. The United States does not draw a nationally representative sample of immigrants from anywhere. If you want to get a sense of how much work has been done and some of the controversies surrounding estimates of national IQ, visit the National IQ Dataset, a site that maintains a curated inventory of the studies of national IQ and posts discussions of many of the technical issues. As of February 2020, I found the releases of the data set at viewoniq.org/?page_id=9, and the discussions at viewoniq.org/.

13. I've been writing about interventions to raise IQ for a long time. For a review of the state of knowledge as of the early 1990s, see Chapter 17 of Richard Herrnstein and Charles Murray, *The Bell Curve: Intelligence and Class Structure in American Life* (1994). For an update through the first half of the 2000s, see Chapter 2 of Charles Murray, *Real Education: Four Simple Rules for Bringing American Education Back to Reality* (2008). For a discussion that incorporates recent developments in the understanding of heritability and the nonshared environment as they relate to early interventions, see Chapter 13 of Charles Murray, *Human Diversity: The Biology of Gender, Race, and Class* (2020). I will not try to summarize the many findings here, but one is so uncontested that it deserves mention: For the vast majority of U.S. children, low scores on cognitive tests are not changed by remedial courses. Much more intensive efforts are required, and even those have produced disappointing results. A few experimental pre-K programs have produced statistically significant gains on exit tests, but these results suffer from fadeout. A good optimistic review of the pre-K literature is Greg J. Duncan and Katherine Magnuson, "Investing in Preschool Programs," *Journal of Economic Perspectives* (2013). A good skeptical review of the evidence is Grover J. Whitehurst, "Does State Pre-K Improve Children's Achievement?" Brookings (July 12, 2018).

14. Each item in a major test is scrutinized for evidence that it is unusually hard for some group – i.e., not just harder for that group than for another group, but harder in relation to other items in the same test. For example, suppose that the group difference runs between 0.6 and 0.8 SDs for 19 out of 20 items on an IQ subtest but is 1.5 SDs on the remaining one. That would be a red flag that

something other than a difference in *g* is affecting the result on that item.

Once a draft of the test passes scrutiny on the individual items, it can be tested for measurement invariance. The technique of choice is multiple-group confirmatory factor analysis. Cognitive tests have complex structures. There are a variety of ways to determine whether the structures are the same for different groups by measuring not only whether the factor structures themselves are similar, but also whether the factor loadings, intercepts, and residual variances are similar across groups. Together, these constitute strong evidence that the test is measuring the same construct for different groups. All the current versions of the major tests are known to be factor invariant.

### CHAPTER 4: RACE DIFFERENCES IN VIOLENT CRIME

1. The exact bases for a legal arrest vary from jurisdiction to jurisdiction, but three are common to all:

    › The police officer personally observed a crime taking place.

    › The police officer at the scene has probable cause to believe that the arrestee recently committed or is about to commit a crime.

    › The police officer has an arrest warrant issued by a judge.

    "Probable cause" means that the police officer has specific, tangible evidence within the officer's knowledge that would lead a reasonable person to think the arrestee is guilty.

    From a social scientist's perspective, an arrest by the police has several advantages as evidence of race differences in crime. Most police do not make arrests lightly, for reasons both professional and practical. With misdemeanors, a warning can often solve a problem without getting the culprit enmeshed in the criminal justice system. With felonies, police are aware how easily a prosecution can get thrown out if there's a problem with "probable cause." Even a completely legal arrest involves a lot of paperwork. From the social scientist's perspective, these disincentives to arrest people give the arrest extra credibility as evidence that a meaningful offense occurred and that the police arrested a plausible suspect.

    Another reason that arrests for violent offenses are especially valuable for assessing race differences in criminal behavior is that they are largely insulated from the usual problems that raise public concern. Much of the criticism of the police involves situations that give police officers considerable latitude in deciding whether to intervene – examples are stop-and-frisk, arrests for minor offenses as part of "broken windows" policing, enforcement of vice laws, and enforcement of drug laws. Given credible evidence that a murder, rape, robbery, or aggravated assault has been committed, there is much less police discretion about whether to act.

It's not just the seriousness of the crimes that sets arrests for violent crimes apart; it's also the circumstances under which those crimes get into the statistics. Police seldom catch offenders in the act of murdering, raping, robbing, or assaulting. Far more commonly, the crimes occur and then come to the attention of the police. The potential for the police to manufacture violent offenses for Africans or Latins while overlooking them for Europeans is constrained.

2. The proper calculation of the arrest rate for any group is to divide the number of arrests by the total number of people in that group in the jurisdiction where the arrests occurred. The *ratio* of two rates is one divided by another. If the Latin arrest rate for some crime is 50 per 100,000 and the Asian arrest rate for that crime is 20 per 100,000, the Latin/Asian ratio of rates is $50 \div 20$, or 2.5 to 1.

Just about every arrest rate by race you have ever seen in print or on television has been presented in terms of the percentage of arrests of a given race relative to that race's percentage of the national population. If Latins are 18 percent of the population but they account for 27 percent of the arrests for violent crime (as in the FBI statistics for 2019), it looks as if the disproportion amounts to $27 \div 18$, or 1.50, meaning that Latins were arrested 50 percent more often than their proportion of the population would predict.

The problem is that Latins – and Africans and Asians as well – are not spread evenly around the country. To see why this is important, imagine a nation with a majority population of 1,000,000 and a minority population of 50,000. A member of the majority was arrested 5,000 times last year. A member of the minority was arrested 2,000 times.

The total number of arrests in this nation last year was 7,000. So a newspaper story reads: "Minority accounts for 29 percent of the arrests despite being less than 5 percent of the population. That's a ratio of 6 to 1." That is the usual arithmetic behind reports of race differences in arrest rates. It's not arithmetically wrong, but how meaningful is it?

If every jurisdiction in the country has precisely the national percentages of majority and minority, it's meaningful. But as it happens, my fictional nation consists entirely of rural countryside with the exception of a single city inhabited by 50,000 of the majority and all 50,000 of the minority. So the city experienced 250 arrests of members of the majority last year (its fair share of the 5,000 arrests of the majority) and all 2,000 of the arrests of the minority. That means the minority accounted for 89 percent of the arrests in the city, or a ratio of 2,000 to 250, which equals 8 to 1.

For everyone outside the city, the 6 to 1 national ratio is meaningless in terms of their own lives. If an arrest occurs where they live, the probability that it was committed by a member of the minority is not 89 percent. It is zero. The city is the only place in the country where race differences in arrest rates are relevant, and the relevant ratio is 8 to 1.

Such problems are common when statistics are aggregated. Suppose you wanted to investigate gender discrimination in a university's faculty and based your conclusions on all the departments combined. The patterns you observe in the university as a whole could be radically different from those in either the physics department or the sociology department. The kinds of mistakes I'm describing are sometimes grouped under the label "ecological fallacy."

3. For a list of cities and counties with Open Data sites, see data.gov or https://opendatainitiative.github.io/. I found the thirteen cities by checking each of the 200 largest American cities for an Open Data file of arrest records and conducted additional searches that identified a few smaller jurisdictions with downloadable arrest records. A fourteenth city, Dallas, has released its arrest records but they have been purged of all arrests for murder and rape, making the Dallas statistics incomparable with those of the other thirteen.

Getting from the raw data in the downloadable databases to arrest rates required all the usual steps involved in cleaning databases plus a crucial additional one: identifying the arrests that qualify as arrests for index crimes under the UCR criteria.

The Chicago database of arrests had a variable that explicitly classified arrests as index crimes under the FBI definition. For the other twelve cities, I used variables that classified arrests according to the legal definitions used in their jurisdiction. For most crimes, this was not a problem. Arrests for homicides in all thirteen cities discriminated between murder and various degrees of manslaughter. Arrests for serious assaults were usually described with the word *aggravated* or by other details that qualified the assault as aggravated (e.g., *ADW*, meaning assault with a deadly weapon). For databases that classified a crime by 1st degree, 2nd degree, or 3rd degree, I looked up the legal definition for that jurisdiction to determine which categories would qualify under the FBI definition.

The crime that proved hardest to classify confidently was theft. The official FBI definition does not specify a dollar value, implying that even the most minor thefts could qualify. The arrest databases almost always had subcategories of theft defined by the dollar value. I designated a given arrest as an index theft using a combination of minimum value (usually $500) and police classification of the theft as a felony.

I am sure that my decision rules did not perfectly identify the set of arrests that each police department submitted to the UCR, but I am confident that the overlap is extremely high. Moreover, there is no reason to think that the misclassified arrests would tend to overestimate or underestimate arrests by race.

4. Fayetteville broke out Latins as a separate category, but the Fayetteville database also included the name of each arrestee. Upon examination, it was apparent that many people with Latin names had not been classified as Latin. I'm not referring to borderline names that might possibly be Latin, but rather to names such as Gonzalez or Gomez. I attempted to prepare corrected numbers of Latin arrests, but going solely by names is too inaccurate, so I decided not to report a Latin rate for Fayetteville. I have no idea what the correct number might be.

5. Stewart D'Alessio and Lisa Stolzenberg, "Race and the Probability of Arrest," *Social Forces* (2003), p. 1381. A little history will help set the context of the quotation.

One of the first systematic analyses of crime, based on delinquency among the entire birth cohort of males born in Philadelphia in 1945, found that the rate of contacts of juveniles with the police was 139.9 per 1,000 for non-Whites and 9.2 per 1,000 for Whites – a ratio of 15.2. See Marvin E. Wolfgang, Robert M. Figlio, and Thorsten Sellin, *Delinquency in a Birth Cohort* (1972). That was an unpopular finding in the 1970s, when the conventional wisdom among sociologists was that race differences in crime were an artifact. Their position was supported by self-report studies of criminal behavior that found only minor race differences. See Jay R. Williams and Martin Gold, "From Delinquent Behavior to Official Delinquency," *Social Forces* (1972); and Martin Gold and David Reimer, "Changing Patterns of Delinquent Behavior among Americans 13 through 16 Years Old," *Crime and Delinquency Literature* (1975).

Then in 1978, the criminologist Michael Hindelang published a landmark study in which he compared arrest data to victimization surveys. His conclusion:

> These [victimization] data for rape, robbery, and assault are generally consistent with official data on arrestees and support the differential involvement hypothesis. Some evidence of differential selection for criminal justice processing is found; however, most of the racial disproportionality in arrest data is shown by victimization survey data to be attributable to the substantially greater involvement of blacks in the common law personal crimes of rape, robbery, and assault. These results suggest that traditional admonitions against using arrest data as an index of involvement in these crimes may be overly cautious. (Hindelang, "Race and Involvement in Common Law Personal Crimes," *American Sociological Review* (1978), p. 93.)

Hindelang's findings guided criminologists for the next thirty years, with some 160 studies citing him to justify the use of arrest data as a surrogate measure of criminal offending. The D'Alessio and Stolzenberg study in 2003 took advantage of a new database, the National Incident-Based Reporting System, to reinvestigate the issue with a more rigorous research design than was possible with the data that Hindelang had had to work with. The authors used multivariate logistic regression to calculate the probability of arrest after taking several independent variables into account. The independent variables included (among others), the race, sex, and age of both the victim and the offender, whether the victim was injured, whether a deadly weapon was used, the relationship between the victim and the offender, and the location of the crime. The objective of the analysis was to test whether, given that the race of the offender was identified, Black citizens have a higher probability of being subjected to arrest than White citizens. The quotation in the text continued with this conclusion: "These findings suggest that the disproportionately high arrest rate for black citizens is most likely attributable to differential involvement in reported crime rather than to racially biased law enforcement practices." That's where the science on this issue still stands as I write.

6. According to Africans who reported crimes, the African/European ratio of alleged perpetrators was 82.9 and the Latin/European ratio was 8.3. According to Latins who reported crimes, the African/European ratio of alleged perpetrators was 14.9 and the Latin/European ratio was 26.3.

7. The emphasis that police departments put on identifying "hot spots" plus the ease with which police can use a mapping app to get GPS coordinates has led many departments to include GPS coordinates for the arrest as part of the arrest record. These in turn can be reverse-geocoded to yield the zip code in which the arrest fell. I should add that care must be taken in curating these data – apparently, arresting officers often record the GPS coordinates of the police station where the suspect was booked rather than the location of the crime, and local jails generate a disproportionate number of charges of inmates that are recorded as arrests. The reverse geocoding for my databases was done by Texas A&M Geoservices (https://geoservices.tamu.edu/).

## CHAPTER 5: FIRST-ORDER EFFECTS OF RACE DIFFERENCES IN COGNITIVE ABILITY

1. In the 2020 *SAT Suite of Assessments Annual Report*, downloadable at collegeboard.org, the table titled "SAT Participation and Performance: Score Distributions by Subgroup" gives the percentage of test takers who scored 1400–1600 by race and the total number of test takers, providing an estimate of the number of test takers in the 1400–1600 range by race. It is a very imprecise estimate for Africans because the College Board rounded percentages to the nearest whole point. The 1 percent reported for African students could be anywhere from a maximum of 1.49 percent to a minimum of 0.5 percent – 50 percent too small or 50 percent too high. I assumed 1.0 percent in making my calculations.

The College Board also reported the mean and SD for each race. Combining these two sets of information and applying the

mathematics of a normal distribution, it was possible to reach estimates for numbers of students with SAT scores of 1500 or higher.

2. The online documentation has more on this issue, but to give you
a sense of how quickly the pool of approximately 900 African
applicants with scores of 1500+ would be depleted, just six schools
in the *US News* top 25 universities for 2020 – Harvard, Yale, Penn,
Columbia, Duke, and Johns Hopkins – had about 950 African
freshmen in 2019. As for the approximately 3,300 Latins with
such scores, 19 of the 25 top-rated universities had 3,360 Latin
freshmen. In all, the top 25 universities had about 3,650 African
freshmen and 8,650 Latins. We can be sure that virtually every
African or Latin applicant with a 1500+ score was admitted with a
full financial ride if they applied to one of those schools, and that
an extremely high proportion of them accepted.

To give you a sense of how many well-regarded schools are left
with few or no African or Latin applicants with scores of even 1200
(about the 76th percentile for the 2020 SAT) or above, the numbers of African and Latin applicants with scores of 1200+ were
about 20,900 and 68,300 respectively. The numbers of African
and Latin freshmen in the top 100 *US News* universities were
22,440 and 56,881 respectively. In other words, given perfect top-
down matches of university rank with African and Latin SAT
scores, the top 100 universities could have soaked up more than all
of the African students with scores of 1200+ and 83 percent of
Latin applicants with scores of 1200+. More than two-thirds of all
high school graduates who enter four-year colleges do not attend
one of those top 100. (In 2019, 438,000 students entered the top
100 as first-year students while total first-year enrollment for all
four-year colleges and universities was about 1.4 million.)

3. The evidence for the summary statements in the text is given
below. Sources are provided in the online documentation.

*Pass Rates for Bar Examinations.* A large-scale study in the
1990s found that the pass rates for persons taking a bar exam for
the first time were 92 percent for Europeans, 81 percent for Asians,
75 percent for Latins, and 61 percent for Africans. The only more
recent data I have been able to find, for a 2020 administration of
the California bar exam, found much lower pass rates of 52 percent
for Europeans, 31 percent for Latins, and 5 percent for Africans.

*Client Complaints about Attorneys.* A 2019 study of complaints
lodged with the California Bar Association among attorneys

admitted to the bar from the 1990s to 2009 found the following percentages of attorneys who had been the subject of ten or more formal complaints and who had been disciplined with temporary or permanent suspension of their license to practice law.

| | California Attorneys | | | |
| --- | --- | --- | --- | --- |
| | European | African | Latin | Asian |
| Attorneys with 10+ Complaints Lodged | 2.8% | 7.2% | 5.0% | 2.0% |
| Attorneys Placed on Probation | 0.6% | 1.9% | 1.2% | 0.4% |

The African/European ratios for 10+ complaints and suspended licenses were 2.5 and 3.0 respectively and the corresponding Latin/European ratios were 1.8 and 1.9. The African/Asian ratios for 10+ complaints and suspended licenses were 3.5 and 4.3 respectively and the corresponding Latin/Asian ratios were 2.5 and 2.8. Note that Europeans had more investigations than Asians. The European/Asian ratios for 10+ complaints and suspensions were 1.4 and 1.5 respectively.

*Board Certifications for Medical Specialties.* Board certification in a medical specialty is not associated with large differences in quality of care, but physicians have strong professional incentives to become board-certified. Some patients searching for a new physician use board certification as one of their criteria. Many hospitals and managed-care organizations require board certification. It's not a demanding standard – more than 80 percent of physicians in specialties are board-certified – but *not* getting certification despite the normal incentives to do so is a negative indicator.

A study of all U.S. medical school graduates from 1997 to 2000 followed them through eight years after graduation. The study reported the percentage of physicians practicing in eight specialties who had obtained board certification broken down by White, Asian/Pacific, and "underrepresented minorities," defined as Blacks, Hispanics, and Native Americans. Aggregating across all eight specialties, 11.1 percent of Whites and 12.1 percent of Asian/

Pacific physicians were not board-certified, compared to 21.9 percent of underrepresented minorities.

*Patient Complaints about Physicians.* The Medical Board of California is the state agency for licensing and regulating physicians. A study of complaints, investigations, and discipline from July 2003 to June 2013 found the following proportions by race:

|  | California Physicians | | | |
|---|---|---|---|---|
|  | European | African | Latin | Asian |
| Physicians with Complaints | 28.0% | 43.0% | 36.5% | 24.7% |
| Physicians with Investigations | 6.7% | 11.7% | 9.7% | 5.3% |
| Physicians Disciplined | 1.0% | 1.5% | 1.9% | 0.8% |

These three indicators are roughly analogous to reports of crimes, arrests, and sentences in Chapter 4, with investigations probably being a better indicator than complaints or discipline for the same reason that arrests are a better indicator than reported crimes or sentences. Reported complaints and investigations follow the familiar ordering high to low – Africans, Latins, Europeans, and Asians. The African/European ratio was 1.7 and the Latin/European ratio was 1.4. Europeans had more investigations than Asians. The European/Asian ratio was 1.3.

*Pass Rates on the Certified Public Accountant (CPA) Examination.* The CPA exam is a sixteen-hour test administered in four separate sections. Passing the CPA exam is not required to work as an accountant, but is necessary for anyone who hopes to rise in the field. Most people take the exam from their late 20s through early 30s. The table below shows three results for CPA candidates from 2005 to 2016.

The European/African pass ratio was 2.3. The European/Latin ratio was 1.5. For the two types of dropout – those who did not reattempt the exam after failing and those who stopped after the first of the four sections – the African/European ratios were 2.5

CPA Candidates, 2005–2016

|  | European | African | Latin |
|---|---|---|---|
| Passed all four sections | 47.7% | 20.2% | 31.9% |
| Dropped after first attempt | 7.7% | 19.2% | 15.0% |
| Dropped after first section | 2.0% | 4.6% | 3.8% |

and 2.4 respectively. The corresponding Latin/European ratios were 1.9 and 2.0.

*High-Stakes Ratings of K–12 Teachers.* Michigan enacted a law mandating high-stakes ratings of teachers in 2011. From 2011 to 2015, 2.2 percent of European teachers were rated "minimally effective" or "ineffective" compared to 4.6 percent of Latin teachers and 7.5 percent of African teachers. This amounts to an African/European ratio of 3.4 and a Latin/European ratio of 2.1 The same pattern applied to teachers who received multiple ratings of "minimally effective" or "ineffective" over the five-year period. The African/European ratio was 3.2 and the Latin/European ratio was again 2.1.

# Index

abolitionism, 2

achievement tests, 21–22, 27; bias or predictiveness in, 24–25, 42–46; comparative results, 33–37; *g*-loading in, 28, 29, 133; longitudinal studies, 28–30; and school reform, 25–26; *see also* cognitive (IQ) tests

ACT test, 30, 43, 46; comparative results, 67, 69–70

affirmative action, 67–71, 120–22; and anti-Asian discrimination, 69

Albuquerque, NM, 89

American Community Survey (ACS), 9, 11–12, 87, 129

American creed, 1–8, 123–25

*American Dilemma, An* (Myrdal), 2

American Psychological Association, 43–45

AncestryDNA, 10

antidiscrimination law, 79, 85, 87, 122; Civil Rights Act (1964), 3–4, 23

Armed Forces Qualification Test, 28, 85

Armed Services Vocational Aptitude Battery, 85

arrest rates, 49–52; calculation of, 137–38; for murder, 53–56; for property crime, 61–62

Asheville, NC, 50, 51, 56, 61

Bailyn, Bernard, 122–23

Baltimore, MD, 50, 51. 56, 61

*Bell Curve, The* (Herrnstein/ Murray), 25, 36; controversy over, 43; and outliers, 112; and Red Book data, 68–69

Bennet, James, 108

*Bias in Mental Testing* (Jensen), 24–25

Biden, Joe, 6, 7–8, 114, 124

Black Lives Matter protests (2020), 5, 59, 106; and White guilt, 117

*Black-White Test Score Gap, The*, 25

Bobko, Philip, 84

Bush, George W., 25

California Bar Association, 143

Capitol siege (Jan. 6), 7–8, 119

Census Bureau, 9, 11–12

Center for American Progress, 128

Certified Public Accountant (CPA) exam, 80, 86, 144–45

Chandler, AZ, 50, 51, 56, 61

Charleston, SC, 50, 51, 56, 61

Chetty, Raj, 93

Chicago, 17, 24, 91; crime rates in, 50–52, 56, 61

childcare workers, 76, 78–79

churches, 99

Civil Rights Act (1964), 3–4, 23

civil rights movement, 2–3

# A NOTE ON THE TYPE

FACING REALITY *has been set in Monotype Bulmer. Based on types cut by William Martin in 1790, Bulmer builds on the structure of Caslon but anticipates the stronger geometry and dramatic contrast of stroke found in the types cut by Bodoni and the Didots. Like Baskerville and Bell, its close contemporaries, Bulmer looks best on a smooth sheet, a fact that no doubt contributed to the popularity of American Type Founders' 1928 revivial of the face. ‡‡ Bulmer is notable for its upright carriage and its strong color on the page. The italic is equally strong in color, yet provides a decorative quality that makes a fine counterpoint to the formality of the roman.*

DESIGN & COMPOSITION BY CARL W. SCARBROUGH